COLLECTOR'S GUIDE TO AMERICAN WICKER FURNITURE

COLLECTOR'S GUIDE TO AMERICAN WICKER FURNITURE

RICHARD SAUNDERS

HEARST BOOKS · NEW YORK

Library of Congress Cataloging in Publication Data

Saunders, Richard, 1947–
    Collector's guide to American wicker furniture.

    Includes bibliographical references and index.
    I. Wicker furniture—United States—Collectors and collecting.   I. Title.
    TT197.7.S39   1983   749.213   82-23387
    ISBN 0-87851-307-8

10 9 8 7 6 5 4 3 2 1

Printed in the United States of America

for Paula and Mary Jean

ACKNOWLEDGMENTS

The author wishes to thank the following antiques dealers for their generous assistance: Mary Jean McLaughlin of "A Summer Place" in Guilford, Connecticut; Frank H. McNamee of "The Wicker Porch" in Wareham, Massachusetts; Charlie and Steve Wagner of "The Wicker Lady" in Newton Highlands, Massachusetts; Edith Langfur of "Cubbyhole Antiques" in Nyack, New York; Merry and Jerry Gilbert of "Frog Alley Wicker & Antiques" in New Lebanon, New York; Michon Gentray and Christa Carlson of "Wisteria Antiques" in Santa Cruz, California; Jim and Marian Redmond of "The Wacky Wicker Workers" in Mentor, Ohio; Judy Sikorski of "Wickering Heights" in Rossford, Ohio; Bill and Lee Stewart of "The Collected Works" in Wilmette, Illinois; Rose and Walter Kurzmann of "Turn O' the Century Antiques" in Montgomery, New York; "Jean Newhart's Antiques" in Los Gatos, California; and Ralph Lossino of the Montgomery Auction Exchange in Montgomery, New York.

I would also like to acknowledge the cooperation of the staffs of the Wakefield Historical Society in Wakefield, Massachusetts; the Mark Twain Memorial in Hartford, Connecticut; the Lucius Beebe Memorial Library in Wakefield, Massachusetts; the Levi Heywood Memorial Library in Gardner, Massachusetts; the Atlanta Historical Society; the Worcester Historical Museum in Worcester, Massachusetts; the University of Texas Humanities Research Center in Austin; the California Historical Society in San Francisco; the Museum of Fine Arts in Springfield, Massachusetts; and *Americana* magazine.

Last, I'd like to thank the following individuals for their kind help in contributing a good deal of their time and effort to this book: Dorothy Mack for her valuable research, Fran and Mary McNamee, Luba Zuber for her editorial assistance, Katherine Woodward Mellon, Mrs. Thomas McDermott, Miss Margaret Hays for her sense of direction, Mrs. Elaine Disick, Ruth Woodbury, Don Lynch, and Phyllis Haders for her collection of antique quilts.

Special thanks to the Wagner Airport Limousine Service of Boston.

CONTENTS

COLLECTOR'S GUIDE TO
AMERICAN WICKER FURNITURE

❧ 1 ❧

THE WICKER REVIVAL

Wicker furniture, the woven wonder of a bygone era, is enjoying an unprecedented renaissance in the antiques field. Back in fashion since the 1960s, fine antique wicker now seems destined for greater popularity than ever before. From the flights of fancy in design that made handmade Victorian wicker exotic and romantic to the less imaginative but practical machine-made pieces of the 1920s, collectible wicker furniture is now one of the most sought-after items on today's antiques market.

Gone are the days when the public thought of wicker as being strictly "outdoor" or "porch" furniture. Although a few people still cling to the myth that wicker was made primarily for outdoors, even the Victorians of the 1880s readily accepted wicker reception chairs, vanities, baby cribs, and piano stools—all designed for indoor use. Furthermore, by 1915 wicker lamps and even wicker phonograph cabinets were flooding the market.

From wicker furniture's first appearance on the marketplace, nineteenth-century Americans fell in love with it. It captured the mood of the times to a "T," reveling in the adoration of the home

A fanciful lyre-backed lady's reception chair and a rare double-shelf music stand are samples of styles from the late 1880s.

3

as an island of refuge that celebrated any handmade or eclectic decoration. Possessing more than a hint of Victorian elegance, pre-1900 wicker added an uncommon blend of informality and dimension to any room in the home. Light, airy, and exotic, the elusive qualities of wicker furniture somehow captured the leisurely pace of the day while at the same time adding a touch of Oriental mystery. It had fantasy value.

After the Victorian era or "Golden Age of Wicker," the art of woven furniture survived because of its inherent adaptability. It managed to continue catering to both the romantic and practical sides of human nature during the early 1900s' great social change. Wicker maintained its popularity by combining its exotic reputation with the emerging conservative, no-nonsense designs of Gustav Stickley's Mission-style furniture.

Today the public is finally beginning to realize that the superior craftsmanship involved in creating handmade wicker furniture assures its reputation as a true art form. Over the past decade interior decorators have relied on its individual and organic look to lighten rooms while adding an air of nostalgia. Yet the biggest reason for the surprising comeback lies in the fact that each handmade antique piece is a one-of-a-kind object. Nothing was stamped out on an assembly line. Highly skilled wickerworkers labored two or three days to produce one armchair. Every craftsman added his own special touch. A great deal of personal satisfaction and pride went into the making of this wicker. Today's collector senses this pride in the finished product.

What Is Wicker?

With the wicker renaissance on the upswing, it is surprising to discover that many people do not know what wicker is. Although Webster defines it as "a small pliant twig," the term *wicker* has evolved into a generic classification that covers all woven furniture made from natural (and sometimes synthetic) materials. Through the years there has been a great deal of confusion about the term; many people consider wicker a type of material in itself. What they are usually talking about is reed, rattan, fiber, or any number of other materials. Believed to be of Swedish origin (*wika*, to bend, and *vikker*, meaning willow), the term *wicker* only came into widespread use in this country after the turn of the century. In fact, almost all pre-1900 trade catalogues of wicker furniture used the terms *rattan* or *reed* to describe their products.

The most commonly used materials that went into the construction of collectible (pre-1930) wicker furniture are described below.

Rattan

Rattan, which contributes the largest amount of material used in the making of wicker furniture, is derived from the rattan palm. Reed and cane are byproducts of rattan. While there are hundreds of species of rattan palms throughout the East Indies and Southeast Asia, *Calamus rotang*, which thrives in the lush jungles and swamplands of Borneo and the Malay Archipelago, is considered the finest variety for commercial use. More like vines than palms, the stalks of these plants (which rarely exceed a width of an inch and a half) can attain heights of six hundred feet. The vines wind up neighboring trees by means of sharp reversed thorns on the underside of the leaf stalks. After the cut rattan is allowed to dry, its thorny leaves are removed with razor-sharp knives, leaving a highly polished, straw-colored material that resembles young bamboo. Yet rattan lacks the hollow center and characteristic ridge joints that distinguish bamboo. The long vines are cut into sections, gathered into "hanks," and collected by traders for shipment.

Cane

Cane is produced by splitting off the outer bark of whole rattan in thin strips. It is well known as the resilient and glossy material that has been used in the openwork weaving of seats and backs of chairs since the seventeenth century. Cane was also used as the material for set-in cane seats that were prewoven on looms as early as the 1870s. Since the 1840s, binder cane (a slightly wider variety) has been used to wrap the framework of wicker furniture.

Reed

Reed constitutes the central core of whole rattan after the outer covering of cane has been removed. This inner-pith of the rattan palm revolutionized the wicker furniture industry in the 1850s due to its highly flexible nature. Reed could only be cut into various sizes and lengths to fit manufacturers' requirements, as well as cut into round, oval, and flat varieties. It is the most common material used in the construction of collectible wicker furniture. Unlike whole rattan or cane, reed can be stained or painted easily because of its porous nature.

(Note: Reed from the rattan palm should not be confused with swamp reed used in the construction of ancient wicker furniture from Egypt, Rome, or medieval England.)

Willow

Willow, a highly flexible and versatile weaving material, comes from willow trees and shrubs. Willow holts were once harvested specifically for the wicker industry. When the demand for quality willow increased in the early 1900s, it was planted and cultivated as a farm crop for various wicker manufacturers. Hard to distinguish from reed, these blonde-colored twigs, sometimes called *osiers*, often exhibit tiny knots where the offshoots have been removed. Willow, which was used in the construction of many antique wicker pieces, is still popular because of its ability to take both stains and paint well.

Fiber

Often called *art fibre* and *fibre reed*, fiber is a synthetic material made of machine-twisted paper. Introduced during World War I by Marshall B. Lloyd, the material was chemically treated to resemble real twisted bull rushes. Soft and pliable in their original state, many of these "fibre reeds" were twisted around wire centers and used at stress points in the design to ensure durability.

Oriental Sea Grass

A natural, twine-like material, Oriental sea grass (often called "China sea grass" in the past) is hand-twisted to resemble rope; it exhibits a variegated green and tan color and is twisted into various thicknesses.

Prairie Grass

Prairie grass is a natural straw-like material used in some 1910–1930 wicker pieces. It closely resembles Oriental sea grass but does not have the durable qualities of other wicker materials.

Raffia

Raffia is a coarse fiber cut from the leafstalks of the raphia palm of Madagascar. Raffia found limited use in the wrapping of post-Victorian wicker furniture.

Rush

Rush is a natural, grasslike, leafless stem derived from the sedge family. A perennial plant, rush was a little-used material employed in the weaving of pre-1910 wicker.

Woven furniture made from any of the mentioned materials (or any combination of these) can be called wicker furniture.

WICKER THROUGH THE AGES

Ancient Wicker Artifacts

In 1922, the unearthing of the tomb of Egyptian King Tutankhamen from the fourteenth century B.C. created headlines around the world. Newspapers proclaimed it "the greatest archeological discovery of all time." Everyone read about Lord Carnarvon's discovery beneath the huge boulders, limestone chippings, and ancient workmen's huts of Rameses VI's tomb. Carnarvon and his American assistant, Howard Carter, had crawled painstakingly through black passageways with a single flickering candle. Their flame illuminated fantastic statues, "colossal gilt couches," and alabaster artwork that had survived the ravages of time in the air-tight tomb of the boy king. Understandably, the jeweled statues, elaborate furniture employing huge quantities of precious metal, and the solid gold inner coffin bearing the likeness of the king overshadowed the more modest and utilitarian artifacts. Among the more practical, everyday objects were wicker stools made of swamp reed, wicker boxes, and mats woven from rush.

Several centuries before the reign of King Tut, basket weaving—the forerunner of more sophisticated wicker works—was one

Seventeenth-century Dutch artist Samuel Dirksz van Hoogstraten's oil painting, "The First Born," reveals a wicker cradle remarkably like the one brought to America on the Mayflower in 1620.

of the most widespread of activities. Older than cloth weaving and pottery making, the weaving of twigs and swamp reed into wickerwork goes back as far as chipping of flints into arrowheads by Neolithic man. Therefore, it should be no great surprise that the Egyptian basketry tradition utilized local palm, grasses, and rush from as far back as 4000 B.C. Gradually the art developed to include larger wickerwork items such as woven rush mats, coffins, and much later, wicker furniture. The advantages of using wickerwork furniture were recognized early: the material could be woven in much the same way as a piece of basketry and resulted in a lightweight, flexible form that conformed to the shape of the body.

Probably the earliest example of ancient wicker furniture can be traced back to a carved stone pillar marking the grave of a Helwan priestly official, Menka-Heqet (c. 2800 B.C.). A stone relief pictures a primitive seat represented as a solid block scored with a number of vertical lines. According to the late Hollis S. Baker, noted authority on ancient furniture, "This type [of stool] is thought to have served as the model for the hieroglyphic sign ▦ , the yellow color and detail found on early examples of this sign suggesting that such stools were originally made of reedwork."*

Through stone carvings and hundreds of painted tomb scenes we now know that woven reed hassocks date back to 2600 B.C.; reed cosmetic boxes often took the place of heavier wooden boxes around 2000 B.C., and simple woven chests and tables made of woven reed, rush, and twisted papyrus began appearing before 1400 B.C. Interestingly, most of these ancient wicker artifacts exhibit many of the same methods of construction (such as under-and-over weaving techniques, joints wrapped with flat reed, and open latticework) that were used in the making of handmade wicker furniture some 3,000 years later.

*Hollis S. Baker, *Furniture in the Ancient World: Origins and Evolution, 3100-475 B.C.* (New York: Macmillan, 1966), p. 31.

Relief carving on the tombstone of ancient Egyptian Menka-Heqet (c. 2800 B.C.) is now considered by historians to be the earliest example of wicker furniture.

The Roman Empire and Beyond

While our knowledge of homemade wicker furniture from ancient China and Greece is limited to a handful of stone carvings and paintings, the Roman Empire has given us a valuable written record of early wicker furniture. In his *Natural History* Pliny speaks of a type of willow twig that, after the bark is peeled off, "admits of various utensils being made of it, which require a softer and more pliable material than leather: this last is also found particularly useful in the construction of those articles of luxury, reclining chairs."

The ancient art of wattling (a basic type of wickerwork using sticks intertwined with willow twigs) was practiced for centuries by Romans. Aside from wicker furniture, willows were also pains-

takingly cultivated for making utensils, baskets, chests, agricul-
tural tools, and small chariotlike carts around the time of Christ.
With this long-standing tradition of fine wickerwork, it is under-
standable that the finest example of ancient wicker furniture is a
stone relief of Roman origin that shows a woman at her toilet and
seated in a high-backed wicker chair.

Although the British had their own modest history of basket
weaving in medieval times, we know that they inherited the concept
of wicker furniture from their Roman conquerors. The basket chair
became England's basic furnishing shortly after the Roman with-
drawal in the fifth century. Sometimes called a "beehive" or "twig-
gen" chair (a British basket weaver was known as a "twiggy"),
they were made of local materials such as peeled willow twigs or
woven rush. Designed with comfort in mind, the basket chair had
a circular, full-skirted base and a gently sloped back rest. With
no more social prestige than a three-legged stool, these chairs were
made and used almost exclusively by peasants. Toward the end
of the medieval period, the design underwent further improve-
ments, offering peasants more comfort in their elasticlike basket
chairs than the kings and noblemen had in their wooden thrones.
Indeed, wickerwork enjoyed a long reign of popularity in Britain,
and even found its way into the writings of Shakespeare, John
Donne, Robert Burns, and Charles Dickens.

By the sixteenth century wickerwork furniture was being made
around the world. Countries enjoying warmer climates made use
of rattan, twisted palm leaves, and swamp reed. Countries in cooler
climates made use of willow twigs, rush, and various dried grasses.
Everywhere wicker was accepted as the "people's furniture"—
unpretentious, light, and homemade with locally available materials. One example from the sixteenth century, the French "guérite,"
is especially noteworthy; the design was reproduced as late as the
early 1900s by some of America's leading wicker furniture companies. It was actually a hooded wicker chair with deep wings that

formed an arched canopy to ward off drafts. Originally designed for the elderly, the guérite (meaning "sentry box") was intended for outdoor use and afforded protection against both sunlight and harsh winds.

Early American Wicker

The first piece of wickerwork in the American colonies arrived, appropriately enough, on the *Mayflower* in 1620. However, the wicker cradle used to rock Peregrine White to sleep is shrouded in mystery. Historians still debate whether it was made in Holland or imported by the Dutch from China. The latter supposition may be more realistic. Trade between China and Western Europe commenced following the Portuguese's establishment of a permanent settlement in 1557 at Macao, not far from present-day Hong Kong. Regardless of the true origin of this famous cradle (now housed at the Pilgrim Hall Museum in Plymouth, Massachusetts), the fact remains: early American wicker furniture played a minor role in the lives of early colonists.

There is little doubt that the settlers brought memories of simple wicker furniture designs and methods of construction. Seventeenth-century American inventories of household goods show that early pieces were limited to basket chairs and cradles. One of the earliest inventories (a will dated February 1639/40) comes from Captain Adam Thoroughgood of Princess Anne County, Virginia, who made note of "one chair of wicker for a child." Captain George Corwin of Salem, Massachusetts, included "1 old wicker chair" in a listing of his household goods in 1684. Finally, in an *Antiques* magazine article on seventeenth-century wickerwork, an account from 1666 mentions "Wicker-Chairs" as part of cargo aboard a New England sailing ship bound for Maryland.*

*Marion Day Inverson, "Wickerwork in the Seventeenth Century," *Antiques* (March 1954), p. 206.

The China Trade

England's East India Company began importing rattan during the early years of the China trade in the 1660s. English and French furniture manufacturers soon discovered that stripping off the glossy cane (the outer skin of whole rattan) produced an extremely resilient and flexible material. It was perfectly suited for weaving the seats and backs of wooden chairs.

Around the time the British took over the Dutch's lead in trading in the mid-1700s, the Chinese made Canton the only port open to foreign trade. The trading season at Canton usually lasted about six months (from midsummer to midwinter), but it was often cut

short because of the onslaught of the unpredictable monsoon season. More obstacles arose when Western traders came under constant surveillance by the Chinese police because of a surge in opium sales. Westerners were restricted to doing business at private residences and at trading headquarters called *hongs*. The hongs were owned by the wealthier merchants of Canton and one of the most coveted honors foreign traders could be given was to be invited to soirées at the homes of these merchants. It was here, in the lavish homes and gardens of successful Chinese merchants, that British and American traders first set eyes on elaborate wicker fantail or "peacock" chairs made of rattan. Many of the chairs were decorated with jewels woven into the fantail back rests, creating the illusion of shining peacock feathers. Traders could hardly resist bringing samples back as curiosity items to their respective countries.

By the mid-nineteenth century the China trade had changed considerably for American traders. With the opening of the Treaty Ports of Hong Kong, Shanghai, Amoy, Foochow, and Ning-po early in the 1840s, the traders began to frequent ports other than Canton and were offered a greater variety of goods. The most important item shipped back to America was neither expensive silks nor exquisite pieces of porcelain, but a rough material used exclusively for securing cargo during the turbulent ocean voyage. The material, whole rattan, soon played a major role in creating a vast American industry.

e Wakefield Rattan Company's ngapore warehouse where employees ocess harvested rattan. The company's 90 trade catalogue explains their ocess: "This work is done principally the native Malays and Chinese olies, and consists of removing, by eans of sand and running water, all icate and other objectionable matter om the surface; after which comes sun eaching, picking, assorting and ndling before the goods are ready to loaded on our ships for Boston."

❧ 3 ❧
VINTAGE WICKER, VICTORIAN STYLE

Cyrus Wakefield

It's hard to believe that a prosperous nineteenth-century business, considered one of America's great success stories, was launched on the strength of a foreign, exotic material used for decades as dunnage aboard clipper ships from the Far East. However, that is precisely how the wicker furniture industry was born.

On the docks of Boston in 1844 a young grocer named Cyrus Wakefield observed a group of volunteers carting bundles of rattan poles off the wharf to eliminate fire hazards. Upon examining some of the long, flexible poles, Wakefield became intrigued and shouldered a bundle of poles back to his waterfront grocery store. Wakefield, who had no previous experience or interest in furniture design, began conducting experiments with the rattan by wrapping provincial-style rocking chairs with the discarded material. Soon he discovered that the rattan became extremely supple when soaked in water and still retained its strength. Years later he was amazed to learn that the Orientals made twisted "rope" out of whole rattan, using it in part for cables and suspension bridges.

Cyrus Wakefield had been born on a farm in Roxbury, New

This 1890s "fancy reception chair" or "photographer's chair" is like dozens of props used in Victorian portrait studios.

Hampshire, in 1811, a world apart from his latter-day pulsating business environment. Because of the limited educational opportunities of the times, Cyrus quit school and left his rural home for the big city at the age of fifteen to seek his fortune in the business world. While employed for three years in a retail grocery store, he attended night schools, pursuing academic and mercantile studies, all the while saving his hard-earned money. In 1834, after years of toil and cautious real estate investments, he entered the grocery business under the firm name of Foster and Wakefield. Two years later the firm was dissolved and Wakefield sent for his younger brother, Enoch, with whom he formed a partnership under the name of Wakefield and Company. After this new enterprise enjoyed several years of success, Cyrus felt secure enough in 1841 to marry Eliza A. Bancroft of Lynnfield, Massachusetts. Three years later his fascination and subsequent experimentation with rattan led him to sell his share of the grocery business to Enoch and embark on a jobbing trade in rattan.

By this time Cyrus Wakefield was literally obsessed with the possibilities of rattan from both a business and an esthetic standpoint. Selling his initial purchases of imported rattan to basket makers and furniture manufacturers (who used the outer covering, or "cane," to weave chair seats), he found his jobbing trade to be lucrative. This gave him the wherewithal to continue his experiments with furniture designs using whole and split rattan. However, because of an increased demand for cane during the late 1840s, Wakefield was forced temporarily to turn his energies to supplying cane in greater quantities to wooden furniture manufacturers. Seeking more rattan, Wakefield sent sample sizes of the cane in demand to his brother-in-law, who was working in Canton at the time. Wakefield asked him whether the cane could be imported from China prestripped, thus saving the cost of hand-stripping the cane from reed in America. Wakefield's brother-in-law sent back good news: prestripped cane was available. Wakefield soon began hiring clipper ships to bring the popular cane, as well as rattan, back to America.

As Cyrus Wakefield's import business became known throughout the United States, he continued experimenting with wicker furniture, creating original designs from frames of hickory or oak. After steaming and bending the wood into flowing shapes, he filled in the frames with rattan fancywork and wrapped them with split cane. Wicker furniture-making was quickly being transformed from a homemade craft into a sophisticated, highly profitable industry. In an effort to increase furniture production, Wakefield and his wife left Boston to establish the Wakefield Rattan Company in South Reading, Massachusetts, in 1855.

Other Early Manufacturers

By the 1850s wicker furniture had caught on with a limited number of other furniture makers in the United States. The work of New York designer John Topf even made it across the Atlantic on display at the Crystal Palace, home of London's Great Exposition of 1851. Another New York firm, J. & C. Berrian, was heralded by writer Gervase Wheeler as the most extensive wicker furniture manufacturer of the day, employing several thousand workers. Although Berrian made standard wicker suites consisting of sofas, armchairs, rocking chairs and foot benches, the company also produced flower stands, cribs, fire screens, and even children's swings. According to Wheeler in his taste manual "Rural Homes," these early designs utilized "firm and delicate braidwork" and relied on the unique properties of rattan: "durability, elasticity, and the great facility of being turned and twisted into an almost endless variety of shapes."

Another company to come out of this period had its roots in the thriving industrial empire of Samuel Colt, who also perfected and produced the repeating revolver. Colt built his sprawling munitions establishment in 1854 less than two miles from the center

Thick reeds and wooden beadwork decorate the top and bottom of this 1880s rocking chair. The standard birdcage design under the arms contrasts with the experimental, open-ended birdcage design on the legs. The odd-shaped, unconventional reed seat completes an extremely rare design.

Famous peacock-design 1880s armchair rests on "birdcage" legs beside an elegant but simple side table from the same period.

of Hartford, Connecticut. Because the location was subject to annual floods, Colt constructed a dike nearly two miles long, planted with German willows to hold the soil in place. Since the willow shoots had to be cut back annually, Colt used the willow crop for the manufacture of wicker furnishings. The Colt Willow Ware Works was added to the armory complex in the late 1850s. Unfortunately, the willowware factory burned down in 1873, and production of wicker furniture never resumed.

Bold Experiment- ation Prompts Industry Rivalry

For the newly formed Wakefield Rattan Company, the 1850s represented an era of great progress. Wakefield continued seeking more pliable materials for his increasingly ornate designs. Eventually he stumbled across a gold mine: reed. This inner pith of rattan was far superior to whole rattan because of its greater flexibility. Until Wakefield's discovery, reed had been treated as waste at furniture factories once the cane was stripped from its outer surface. In addition, reed could be painted or stained, whereas the glossy cane surface of whole rattan resisted any finish but lacquer.

The discovery of reed as a valuable furniture material necessitated a more rapid and economical method than hand stripping the cane from the reed. The American Rattan Company of Fitchburg, Massachusetts, was the only concern that cut cane by machine, but their methods were outdated. Their emphasis was on stripping off the glossy cane for the purpose of creating wooden chair seating rather than on stripping the cane away to get to the newly discovered material, reed. Finally, after using crude cane-splitting machines powered by hand, and later by water, a new steam-driven machine was patented in 1861 by Thomas Mayall (assignor to Cyrus Wakefield). A new era dawned in wicker furniture production.

During the next few years Wakefield and his inventive em-

This rare and elaborately designed swinging crib from the 1880s is popular with collectors because it unpainted, in excellent condition, and has its origin canopy.

ployees developed more impressive methods of mechanically splitting cane. The result: both cane for chair seating and reed for wickerwork could be produced from whole rattan in an instant. Furthermore, a Scotsman in Wakefield's employ, William Houston, single-handedly invented a process of spinning the larger shavings into yarn for table mats, window shades, and floor coverings. Houston was also responsible for a loom (patented in 1870) that wove cane into a webbing to be used like fabric. During the Scotsman's forty-year tenure, his weaving experiments and innovations became so successful that by 1881 fifteen varieties of brush

Top: This rare Victorian library table and matching mirror are enhanced by dried flower and butterfly arrangements pressed under glass. *Bottom:* This square table and the corner chair from 1880 share delicate flowing lines, intricate scrollwork, and artful embellishment—all indicative of the era.

Facing page, top: The golden age of wicker produced fine examples of craftsmanship: an armchair with popular rolled or serpentine arms and a back with fancy weaving in a spiral design; pre-1900 two-tiered, oak-topped table with arched cabriole leg design; and Victorian armchair with unique, closely woven backrest and rolled headrest. *Facing page, bottom:* An early 1890s octopus-like divan from the Wakefield Rattan Company is decorated with a circular sunrise-motif backrest along with waves of curlicues and wooden beadwork. *Above:* Fine craftsmanship produced this mid-1880s armchair with intricate weaving, abundant wooden beadwork, curlicue designs, flowing scrollwork, and a spiderweb caned back panel.

Facing page: This dining room set from the early 1900s, with octagonal table top and mushroom-like woven base, is surrounded by matching dining chairs from the same era. *Left:* This matching armchair and round table from 1910, handmade of fiber, comprise a desirable set because of original factory paint job in green and gold. *Below:* A turn-of-the-century white side table and closely woven gentleman's armchair like these would delight any collector.

Left: This extremely rare six-foot-high wicker china cabinet from the turn of the century displays an extensive amount of beadwork woven on top and at bottom along the skirting. *Below:* This unique wicker portable bar was handmade of reed around 1915 and built on castors for easy movement. A spacious oak-shelved liquor cabinet is revealed when the bar is swung open. *Facing page:* This attractive 1910 reed set is comprised of a highly unusual lamp designed as a planter, a circular ottoman, and a closely woven armchair.

Facing page, top: Wicker doll furniture is hard to come by. These pieces are no exception: an angular doll's standing crib made of reed, a miniature hamper made of closley woven fiber, and a thirteen-inch-high openwork armchair. *Facing page, bottom:* Machine-made 1920s library tables like this one (measuring 20 inches by 60 inches) were used in libraries as well as hallways and behind sofas. *Above:* The semi-circular designed table and upholstered armchair are constructed of synthetic fiber.

A painted set of 1920s wicker made of fiber offers the perfect counterpoint to the existing decor.

This upholstered wicker couch from the mid-1920s exhibits
the popular "diamond design."

Below: This hard-to-find "fold-out" bed with wicker headboard and sides is flanked by two matching table lamps and bedside tables. *Facing page, top:* This two-drawer vanity dates from the 1920s and includes a three-way adjustable mirror and matching low-back chair. Like the vanity and chair, the floor lamp with its unique fringed shade is an investor's dream. *Facing page, bottom:* A 1925 *Good Housekeeping* advertisement features the Kaltex Furniture Company of Michigan, one of the largest manufacturers of machine-woven fiber furniture in the mid-1920s.

Facing page: This ornate piano chair with serpentine back and adjustable seat and the highly prized three-tiered music stand are good examples of wicker specialty pieces, and they are sound investment items. *Above:* Prized wicker pieces fill this collector's dining room: a unique Victorian "cattail" umbrella stand, a turn-of-the-century wood basket, an extremely rare Victorian firescreen with spiderweb cane center panel, a silver-painted rectangular picture frame, a 1910 dining room set with octagonal top, and a large two-drawer buffet with oak top from the early 1920s.

This upholstered 1920s chaise longue comes complete with magazine rack under the left arm. An ornate Victorian table, a mid-1920s library table, and a turn-of-the-century dining set round out an attractive wicker setting.

mats were offered by the Wakefield Rattan Company.

Through the years the keen business mind of Cyrus Wakefield dominated the wicker furniture business. From the early days of importing whole rattan into Boston by wagon to the virtual creation of a multimillion-dollar industry, Wakefield seemed the archetypical man of destiny. Beyond being at the right place at the right time, his assertive character seemed custom-made for the times. And the times had never been better for the introduction of a new and exotic type of furniture like wicker. Adorned with curlicues and arabesques, Victorian wicker furniture was eclectic—an odd mixture of progressive and traditional designs drawn from innumerable sources and combined with motifs of several different periods. Indeed, wicker designs were well-suited to the Victorian age, for the combination of materials (such as rattan, reed, cane, and willow) seemed to mirror the dramatic combination of revival styles—Classical, Rococo, Gothic, Renaissance, Elizabethan, and Turkish. (However, it wasn't until the 1870s that wicker manufacturers began introducing these styles and capitalizing on the Victorian fetish for elaborate scrollwork and flowing lines.)

By the early 1870s Cyrus Wakefield's rattan business was an enormous success. Not only did his factories and storehouses span ten acres of floorage, but he employed more than a thousand South Reading townspeople. Tragically, during a financial crash known as the "Panic of '73" in which thriving businesses failed and personal fortunes evaporated, Cyrus Wakefield died of a heart attack. He must have sensed the fragile state of the economy as well as his health: two weeks before his death he officially incorporated the Wakefield Rattan Company. His death was noted not merely because he was the father of the American wicker industry, but because he was a civic leader and philanthropist of the highest order. South Reading had benefited from his generosity for decades. In fact, when he donated more than $120,000 for a much-needed town hall, the citizens of South Reading unanimously voted to change the town's name to "Wakefield" in his honor. On July 1, 1868, South Reading was officially renamed.

Although Cyrus Wakefield left no children, he had a nephew and namesake, Cyrus Wakefield II. Young Cyrus had served as a representative of the Wakefield Company in Singapore since 1865. Upon his uncle's death he returned home to assume the responsibilities of managing the company. Less than two years later, the newly elected company president made his first acquisition: the American Rattan Company, Wakefield's chief competitor. The subsidiary's Fitchburg plant was shut down in 1878, and all rattan-splitting machinery was transferred to the Wakefield factory. By

A very rare matching settee and armchair from the 1880s have heart-shaped back panels encircled with curlicues and set-in cane seats.

that time the national economy had greatly improved, and the Wakefield Rattan Company prospered once again.

A few years before his death, Cyrus Wakefield had begun selling whole rattan to Levi Heywood, founder of Heywood Brothers and Company of Gardner, Massachusetts—the largest wooden-chair manufacturer in the United States. Levi Heywood had been in the wooden-chair business since 1826, long before he ventured into wicker manufacturing. But by the start of the Civil War, Heywood established a new company with his four brothers. He wasted little time, inventing machines to manufacture wooden chair

These late-Victorian serpentine pieces rely on conservative flowing lines as well as intricate beadwork and curlicues. A heart-shaped back panel dominates the armchair.

seats, patenting a design for a unique tilting chair, and introducing several processes for bending wood. The latter achievement prompted the following response in a letter from Francis Thonet of Vienna, son of the creator of the famed bentwood rocker, after visiting the Heywood factory: "I must tell you candidly that you have the best machinery for bending wood that I ever saw, and I will say that I have seen and experimented a great deal in the bending of wood."*

The Wakefield Rattan Company's success spurred on Heywood Brothers and Company. Fortunately, the firm employed a Gardner A. Watkins, who not only invented a steam-powered loom that wove cane into continuous sheets but also devised an automatic channeling machine that cut grooves around wooden chair seats. When these two inventions were combined in 1867, the new age of prewoven or "set-in" cane seats was born. Thanks to Watkins, Heywood was able to enter the wicker field with significant savings in labor costs. Over the next quarter of a century, Heywood's company fiercely competed with the Wakefield Rattan Company.

Wicker's Meteoric Rise in Popularity

Thousands of visitors to the Philadelphia Centennial Exhibition of 1876 witnessed an international display of arts and crafts that included wicker furniture. "Hourglass" chairs from China sparked the crowd's interest. (Subsequently the hourglass' popularity spread, and the leading wicker companies wasted no time in copying the design.) The Wakefield Rattan Company's furniture captured fairgoers' eyes as well and received an award from the Centennial Exhibition officials "for original design and superior workmanship in furniture, chairs, and baskets."† Praise was also lavished on

---

*Orra L. Stone, *History of Massachusetts Industries*, vol. 2 (Boston, Chicago: S.J. Clarke, 1930), pp. 1853–54.

†Richard N. Greenwood, *The Five Heywood Brothers (1826–1951: A Brief History of the Heywood-Wakefield Company during 125 Years* (New York: Newcomen, 1951), p. 16.

An early 1890s baby carriage from Heywood Brothers and Company employs an odd-shaped, reed-wrapped wooden framework. The strong elliptical front and back springs are typical of almost all Victorian carriages.

A beautiful 1890s matching settee and armchair. Classic serpentine back and arms, hand-caned back panels, and curlicues comprise a very desirable set.

Wakefield's new car seats, with officials referring to them as "durable, cool, clean, and economical."

Wicker furniture for children began its meteoric climb in popularity in the late 1870s because of the nineteenth-century concern for proper ventilation and the sanitary aspects of the material. As early as 1852 Gervase Wheeler wrote about the "lightness, sweetness, and coolness" of a child's wicker bedstead. Bedsteads were only the beginning; by the 1880s children's highchairs and cribs were being produced in huge quantities. However, the darling of the age was the wicker baby carriage, or "perambulator." Offered in a tremendous variety of designs, these carriages were also stained on order (cherry, mahogany, oak, or clear varnish) and came with plush upholstery and a choice of silk or satin parasols. The demand for wicker baby carriages was so enormous between 1880 and 1895 that Heywood Brothers and Company devoted an entire factory to nothing but carriage production. Trade catalogues devoted exclusively to wicker carriages touted the buggies' charm and quality. Many designs that came out of these specialty catalogues were quite unique, especially the rare "twin" carriage designed for two babies with seats facing each other and employing double parasols. Manufacturers ensured the carriage's year-round use by offering runners in winter. For an extra two dollars the 1886 Heywood Brothers and Company catalogue offered runners to convert a carriage into a "baby sleigh."

There are always underlying reasons for the commercial success of any product. According to one study of rattan carriages:

> . . . the popularity reflected a combination of factors. Perhaps the most important of these was the idealized image of childhood that took place late in the 19th century. Children were no longer treated as adults, as they had been, but were venerated for their childlikeness. This changing attitude was translated naturally into rattan creations: the material was extremely adaptable for the fanciful baby carriage designs.*

At this time wicker was also deemed the perfect outdoor furniture. Wealthy Americans were making ritualistic summer migrations to the seaside and mountains in a quest for fresh air. Country living was believed to be the secret of good health. Vacation houses and resorts were built with spacious verandas and special sleeping porches so that inhabitants were exposed to as much country air as possible. Wicker seemed custom-made for country living: not only did it satisfy the concern for proper ventilation, but its weight allowed the owner to move it outdoors with the utmost ease.

*Katherine Menz, "Wicker Furniture," *American Arts and Antiques* (October 1978), pp. 84–91.

Although the leading household advisories stressed wicker's "coolness and comfort" for the summer season and outdoor use, attitudes toward wicker changed rapidly. By the 1890s, the public finally accepted wicker's unique three-dimensional qualities and began using it more and more in hallways, sitting rooms, dining rooms, offices, libraries, and bedrooms.

While most wicker furniture of this era was left in its natural state, (unpainted or stained), a growing segment of the population cried out for the "judicious gilding" of reeds to highlight designs. This gilding of the lily was accomplished by predyeing or painting individual reeds before weaving them into a piece. Called "fancy colored reeds" in the trade catalogues, the colorful combinations of light green, white, red, and gold seemed to jump out at the viewer. An 1883 issue of *Century* magazine featured a Wakefield Rattan Company advertisement that declared, "the new and original

This distinctive square table from the 1880s catches the eye with its uniquely wrapped ball designs on the base and large birdcage ornamentations in the center.

This elegant 45-inch-high stand from the mid-1880s has four oak-topped tiers.

idea of color work is having great success, and meets the popular demand for novelty in fall furnishing."

Moreover, the early 1880s witnessed the public's growing tendency to paint wicker pieces to match a specific décor in the home. As sunlight and indoor plants invaded the Victorian sitting room, wicker accent pieces made of reed were painted white, green, black, gold, and brown.

By the mid-1880s the Wakefield Rattan Company was selling annually more than two million dollars' worth of wicker furniture. With the average cost of a chair falling between four and twelve dollars, this revenue represented a huge quantity of wicker sales— with no end in sight. The Wakefield Rattan Company, Heywood Brothers and Company, and several of their competitors began issuing trade cards to further stimulate sales. These trade cards, about the size of the popular tobacco cards of the 1880–1900 period that featured baseball or theatrical stars, served as company advertisements. Wicker cards displayed attractive catalogue illustrations of popular wicker designs, along with factory and warehouse locations printed below. Other merchandising aims capitalized on the middle-class' unwavering sense of national pride. The bitter Civil War divisions had finally faded into romanticized legends of heroic boys in blue and gray. The wicker furniture industry immediately incorporated the Liberty Bell and American flag motifs into a limited number of woven back rests.

Orientalism and the Wicker Decorating Trend

After the death of Levi Heywood in July 1882, Heywood Brothers and Company (under the direction of Henry Heywood, the founder's nephew) established a third factory location in Chicago. Heywood's actions intensified his company's ever-growing rivalry with Wakefield Rattan Company. Both companies zeroed in on their main market: the middle class. Parlor suites in the midprice range multiplied along with Oriental-style wicker, the latest rage.

These matching side chairs and square table with cabriole legs date back to the 1890s.

An ornate 1880s era square table adorned with Victorian decorations: birdcage designs, curlicues, wooden beadwork, and fancy scrollwork.

Below: This rare Victorian sewing or "work" basket has a storage area shaped like a boat and a circular basket for a pin cushion hanging below.

Below right: Extremely rare decorative wicker firescreens like this one from the 1870s is very desirable for the serious collector because of its age, rarity, and condition.

Orientalism was spreading like wildfire. After influencing decorative arts such as ceramics, silver, and textiles, it invaded the realm of wicker furniture design. The International Exhibition of 1862 in South Kensington, England, marked the beginning of this movement with displays of Japanese decorative arts, merely three years after the opening of Japan to the West. Yet Orientalism was not accepted in the United States until the last quarter of the nineteenth century. The timing could not have been better for the wicker industry. The ornate qualities of Victorian-style wicker were psychologically linked with the Orient since the 1850s. The exotic Far Eastern flavor of wicker furniture—Moorish and Byzantine styles included—captivated the public. Not surprisingly, the del-

icate asymmetry of Japanese art found its way into many 1880 designs—the most notable being the extremely popular Japanese fan motif set into the back panels of many wicker armchairs, rockers, and high chairs of the day.

The wicker of the exotic eighties was drenched in arabesques, arches, and ogees. Madly ornate designs were gold-leafed and draped with Oriental fabrics. Indeed, wicker from this era carried with it a sense of underlying sensuality and even eroticism. For years wicker and beautiful women were teamed in illustrations from novels and advertising. Even the Oriental-style brothel relied on wicker's inherent erotic aura to the degree that the ornate designs were vaguely associated for some time with prostitutes. The in-

Children's and doll's wicker furniture is now eagerly sought by collectors. Shown here are a rare 1890s doll's washstand complete with side towel racks and a round opening on the top shelf for a wash bowl, classic serpentine child's highchair with removable tray, and a rare doll's swing from the 1890s.

famous "Storyville Portraits," a collection of late nineteenth- and early twentieth-century photographs of prostitutes and brothels from New Orleans' famed red-light district offer proof.

Orientalism prevailed through the 1890s. The Victorian obsession with elaborate decoration was reaching a new high and playing more than ever on Oriental themes to create the desired exotic, Eastern flavor. According to contemporary household books and magazines on the market, Oriental accouterments were just

This classic shell-back-design rocking chair from the 1880s remained popular until the turn of the century. The early 1900s ottoman was also a hit because of its versatility as a makeshift plant stand or taboret.

A Heywood Brothers & Company serpentine rocking chair lik this one from the early 1890s is popular among collector because of the sailboat motif woven into the back panel.

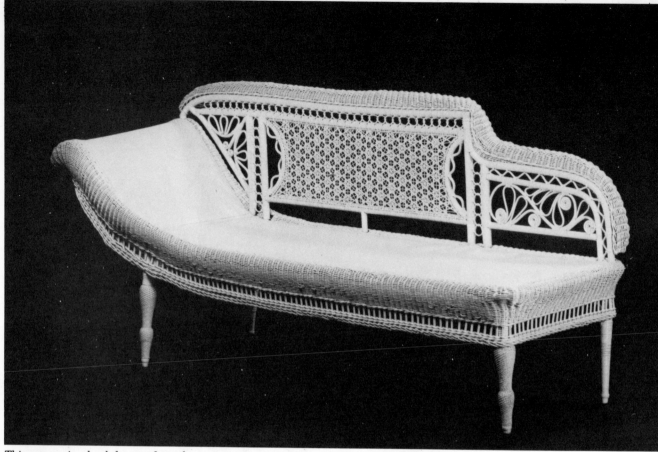

This serpentine-back lounge from the 1890s employs hand caning in the rectangular side panel and prewoven "set-in" sheet for the horizontal seat.

the thing to enhance the allure of wicker. Soon not only were wicker pieces being cushioned with Oriental fabrics, but entire rooms were being decorated with Japanese parasols, paper lanterns, hand-painted fans, and Oriental knick-knacks to create the desired artistic effect. Rooms were being decorated around wicker. Adding to the fire, many well-known artists of the day, among them James McNeill Whistler, Lawrence Alma-Tadema, and William Merritt Chase, were known to furnish their studios with wicker. Popular magazines carried illustrated articles about these famous studios, further popularizing wicker and adding as well to its reputation as "artistic" furniture. And the Victorian housewife was at work, as well, creating fancywork touches of her own: satin ribbons through the intricate weaves, silk tassels and bows at the corners of chairs, and crazy quilts of velvet and silk over the arms of settees.

The Golden Age's Final Days

In a speech commemorating the 125th anniversary of the Heywood Brothers furniture business, Richard N. Greenwood claimed that the last quarter of the nineteenth century found the Wakefield Rattan Company and Heywood Brothers and Company engaged in their most intense competition. According to Greenwood: "Both firms grew at about the same rate, both were known the world over, both were making related products during the last quarter of the century. . . . [If] the historians of this country want an outstanding example of how competition helps to stimulate inventiveness, improves product value, lowers prices, and in general makes business better all around, they might well study the industrial rivalry between Heywood Brothers and Company and the Wakefield Rattan Company."*

As the two giants of the industry were locked in battle, new wicker furniture manufacturers emerged on the scene. Among the best companies were A. H. Ordway and Company of South Farmingham, Massachusetts; Chittenden & Eastman in Burlington, Iowa; Gibbs Chair Company of Kankakee, Illinois; Gendron Iron Wheel Company of Toledo, Ohio; Jones-Smith of New York City; Novelty Rattan Company of Boston; Joseph P. McHugh & Company of New York City; Larkins & Company of San Francisco; and John Wanamaker Company of Philadelphia. Beyond these companies and dozens of other formidable competitors entering the field, the age of the mail-order house was dawning. Montgomery Ward Company, which pioneered the mail-order catalogue in 1872, and Sears, Roebuck and Company, established in 1886, took dead aim at the small-town market. They offered inexpensive wicker through catalogues sent free for the asking. Unfortunately, selections of wicker

*Greenwood, *The Five Heywood Brothers*, p.17.

furniture were limited and of inferior quality in both workmanship and materials.

Despite the economic depression that America faced in the early 1890s, every company's wicker sales flourished, including those of mail-order houses. Good sales were partly the result of modest price ranges and partly attributable to the fact that ornate wicker continued to fill the romantic fancies of the Victorian home-maker. Her every whim was met by a wide assortment of wicker furniture that entered the home: music stands, pie caddies, book-cases, divans, conversation chairs, whatnots, picture frames, piano stools, ottomans, wheelchairs, smoking stands, and even grand-father clocks.

Merger

The Heywood and Wakefield companies, undaunted by the nation's financial woes, maintained their keen competition and produced more wicker furniture than ever before for the 1890s consumer. Business was booming. Then the *New York Times* dropped a bombshell with this front-page headline: "TWO LARGE FIRMS TO MERGE: AN IMPORTANT CONSOLIDATION TO BE MADE IN BOSTON." Details of the surprise merger appeared in the paper's evening edition on March 17, 1897:

> It is announced tonight that the Wakefield Rattan Company will be merged with the firm of Heywood Brothers & Co., thus effecting one of the most important consolidations of capital yet made in New England.
>
> The Wakefield Company manufactures all sorts of rattan goods, including corset stock, and the Heywoods are the most extensive manufacturers of chairs in the United States. The new concern will be the Heywood Brothers & Wakefield Company, and will have a capital of $4,000,000 in 6 per cent cumulative preferred stock, and $2,000,000 in common stock. The business of the combined firms will be prosecuted in all parts of the world.

The deal has been in the air for some months. It has already been ratified by the Heywoods. The annual meeting of the stockholders of the Wakefield Rattan Company will be held here tomorrow and will undoubtedly vote in favor of the consolidation.

Less than a month later the two wicker titans formally incorporated (along with all stock in the closely affiliated Heywood & Morril Rattan Company). The newly formed company was destined to all but monopolize sales of quality wicker furniture for the next two decades. Henry Heywood, the first president of Heywood Brothers and Wakefield Company, realized the vastness of his responsibilities and rose to the challenge. By pooling the top line of craftsmen, furniture designers, and businessmen from both companies he produced the cream of the crop in all three diversified fields. Heywood quickly capitalized on the Wakefield factory cane-weaving machinery with the idea of boosting production of cane seating for electric streetcars. Within a year after the merger he managed to open two new foreign warehouses in London and Liverpool.

The Heywood Brothers and Wakefield Company's consolidation was just in time to bid farewell to the Golden Age of Wicker before the twentieth century arrived with revolutionary wicker designs.

4

OLDTIME PHOTOGRAPHER'S PROPS

Practically every town in Victorian America boasted a photography studio. The proprietor, whether he knew it or not, was an early chronicler of family life. Newborns, graduates, brides, grooms, and entire families posed for the camera—alongside wicker props.

Ornate wicker furniture made its debut in photography studios in the 1870s. Light, airy and noticeably three-dimensional in photographs, wicker props made greater headway in studios during the 1880s and early 1900s. Because it was so inexpensive and easy to store, photographers and the public took wicker to their hearts. In fact, fancy wicker pieces became known as "photographer's chairs." Wicker's popularity in studios created a new market; Heywood Brothers and Wakefield Company featured in their 1898 catalogue an extremely ornate five-legged "posing chair" specifically designed as a photographer's prop. Rare today, these posing chairs were used for their visual effect and were much too narrow for normal use. At twenty-one inches high, the seat was several inches higher than the average wicker chair, and the back was tortuously uncomfortable. Yet, the flowing design and octopus-like curlicues adorning the legs created just the right romantic and exotic mixture.

The following examples of portrait photography using pre-1930 wicker afford a view of various designs from the past and a fanciful glance back to a simpler time.

THE TURN OF
THE CENTURY

A Change
in Tastes

The turn of the century was a time of great transition in the United States. The way people made their living was undergoing a major shift, away from agriculture and toward the rapidly growing world of trade and transportation. Interestingly, the widespread use of home electricity and central heating by the middle class had an indirect but nonetheless substantial effect on the wicker furniture industry. Suddenly, porches across the country were being glassed in and converted into "outdoor rooms" to create spacious family areas and sun parlors. Kept warm by the new hot-air heating systems, these outdoor rooms offered all the modern comforts while still giving the illusion of being outside in a garden. They became a fad that swept the country from 1900 to 1915. Manufacturers quickly adapted to the trend by stepping up production of matching sets that included armchairs, rockers, settees, tables, lounges, ottomans, and increased numbers of plant stands and jardinieres.

The 1900s also brought about a formidable public revolt against Victorian-style wicker furniture. Overnight the flowing and fanciful designs so closely identified with wicker furniture were totally

is natural sewing basket from the
rly 1900s contains an unusual handy
awer for spool thread. Another
conventional aspect of the design is
e solid oak-hinged lid that covers the
rn basket.

rejected and considered gauche. Victorian wicker was abruptly hidden away in attics or barns, hauled to the dump, or used as kindling. For the first time since Cyrus Wakefield's initial 1840s experiments with rattan, the American consumers began buying wicker furniture made outside their own country. Austrian designers and craftsmen gave turn-of-the-century wicker buyers what they wanted: angular, sedate, and straight-lined designs. These restrained and noticeably conservative wicker designs were created through the combined efforts of Austrian architects and artists (among them Hans Vollmer, Kolo Moser, Josef Hoffmann, H. Funke, and Leopold Bauer) and became available as imports in the late 1890s. Aside from the new designs, the American public became fascinated with the use of plush cushioned seats and innovative fabric designs. The Austrians felt that upholstered pieces lent charm and extra comfort to their products. The American consumer approved. Sales of imported Austrian and German wicker skyrocketed while Victorian pieces continued in their drastic decline in popularity. In the meantime, too, the Austrians not only stepped up their production of wicker furniture but cultivated various species of willow, thus ensuring total industrial self-sufficiency.

Not long after the introduction of Austrian wicker imports, Gustav Stickley's "Craftsman" furniture came onto the scene. The Gustav Stickley Company, established in Eastwood, New York, in 1898, began making functional, straight-lined wicker furniture (Mission style) that gave the Austrian designs some competition. Mission style's sturdiness and simple practicality created an immediate sensation. Although Stickley's wicker designs were influenced by earlier Austrian designs and Shaker furniture, his Mission-style wicker had a look and feel of its own. The angular lines and squared-off, boxlike appearance of these willow pieces were distinctly masculine.

Although manufactured in the early 1900s, the design employed in these armchairs goes back to the late 1880s. However, by 1910 simple straight lines such as those utilized in the four-tier pie caddy at center had captured the public's fancy.

Gustav Stickley's oak and wicker work was first shown to the public in 1900 at a trade show in Grand Rapids, Michigan. Although the wicker designs were always of secondary importance to his oak furniture, he later admitted that he underestimated the insatiable appetite in America for sedate wicker. Stickley's energy seemed to know no bounds; in addition to attending to his rapidly growing furniture concern, he was soon voicing his philosophy of spartan decorating and marketing his products via a new service magazine, *The Craftsman*. From the pages of this monthly publication, homemakers could learn how to lighten interiors by the judicious mixing of wood and wicker furniture—all, of course, available from the Gustav Stickley Company.

***

By 1905 the owners of the newly formed Heywood Brothers and Wakefield Company realized that the Mission style was here to stay and produced similar designs. The popular straight-lined look and angular designs gradually replaced the Victorian-style pieces in the company's trade catalogues. With a long, proud history in the wicker industry, the company rose to the challenge and produced unique designs that conformed to current tastes.

After converting to the Mission style, all seemed to be working smoothly at the Heywood Brothers and Wakefield Company. The company kept growing: in 1899 a Buffalo warehouse was established; in 1902 the corporation acquired the plant of the Oregon Chair Company in Portland; in 1913 the Chicago plant was enlarged; and in 1916 the outstanding stock of the Washburn and Heywood Chair Company was purchased. Manufacture of wooden school desks and chairs began along with wooden seats for opera houses and motion picture theaters. The company was expanding its empire.

During the 1900–1910 period the American public had more to choose from than just Stickley or Heywood Brothers and Wakefield Company wicker furniture. The market was filled with new Mission styles offered by plenty of companies: Bielecky Brothers of New York City; Block Go-Cart Company of Philadelphia; Hartford Chair Company of Connecticut; Jenkins-Phipps Company of Wakefield, Massachusetts; Lloyd Manufacturing Company of Menominee, Michigan; the Pacific Coast Rattan Company of San Francisco; and a dozen others.

Imported Wicker and Bar Harbor Designs

Although the Heywood Brothers and Wakefield Company began printing European export catalogues in the mid-1900s, the Vollmer/Prag-Rudmiker Company of Vienna, Austria, and M. A. Nicolai Company of Dresden, Germany, continued successfully importing their fine handmade wicker into America. Other imported

This handsome upholstered armchair and matching ottoman were handmade of willow around 1910. The closely woven style was extremely popular then with the wicker-buying public.

wicker included the ever-popular "Canton Furniture" made by Tung Mow Furniture Company in Hong Kong and imported by A. A. Vantine's of New York City. The largest importer of wicker from the Far East, A. A. Vantine's was advertised as "the Oriental Store" and offered single pieces as well as matching sets of wicker in the hourglass design. Woven in the Orient without a nail in the entire construction, this furniture was lighter than the earlier American pieces because the framework was made of bamboo rather

This is a collector's dream: a museum piece, an oak-topped round table with a revolving bookcase set into the base, made shortly after the merger of the Heywood Brothers and the Wakefield Company in 1897.

The jardinière-type plant stand was one of the most popular wicker designs at the turn of the century when heated "outdoor rooms" and glassed-in porches called for wicker and indoor plants. The Oriental pagoda-style birdcage made of reed is from the 1910 period.

This early 1900s four-wheeled tea cart retains a Victorian taste in design with flowing, beaded wickerwork skirting under the glass-topped serving tray. The bottom shelf is made of oak with closely woven reed skirting.

than hardwood. The Far Eastern flavor surrounding wicker furniture continued influencing sales. Items such as "Hong Kong Club Chairs" were touted as original pieces of furniture "made with all sorts of comfortable hollows that seem to conform to the shape of every kind of figure, and they conduce to a feeling of restfulness not obtainable in chairs of other makes."*

The arts and crafts movement in England, a strong influence on Gustav Stickley's designs, finally gained acceptance in America

*Mary W. Mount, "Furnishing the Porch," *House Beautiful* (May 1913), pp. 184–86.

through Dryad English Cane Furniture imports. Although the early Dryad designs were far less rigid-looking than their Austrian predecessors, their rounded backs and full-length skirting captured a wide import audience. American furniture buyers were fascinated by Dryad's advertising claims that its wicker furniture was "made of the strongest unbleached pulp cane without the use of nails or tacks" and impressed with its sturdy ash framework. Well known as the exclusive importers of this wicker, the company did a brisk mail-order business by offering the illustrated catalogue, "The Dryad Cane Book," free of charge upon request.

During the 1905–1915 period, Mission-style wicker continued to enjoy great success among the American public. However, because of the ever-increasing cost of labor, some manufacturers decided to abandon the costly "Cape Cod" design (an angular yet closely woven style) in favor of an open-weave known as "Bar Harbor." Made in a wide-open pattern of latticework, the Bar Harbor design attracted a lot of attention and soon became an alternative to the strict and somewhat confining lines dictated by the Mission style. Still clean and simple of line, Bar Harbor wicker, along with new Southampton and Newport designs, shared the spotlight with Mission styles. (Huge quantities of wicker were put to use in famous grand hotels and country clubs and assumed the names of various well-known resort spots.) Peeled willow was increasingly used in these new designs. While reed was still the material most often used, willow was in far greater use than ever before. Three species of willow—the American green, the Lemley, and the purple—were planted in holts in the northeastern United States around this time and proved to be extremely beneficial financially.

Experiments were conducted successfully with Oriental sea grass and prairie grass. In addition to the availability of these alternative materials, the advent of fiber in 1904 was a boon to the industry. A tough but highly pliable twisted paper, fiber was

From left to right, a 1915 closely woven design, an ornate early 1900s design complete with curlicues and wooden beadwork, and a 1910 angular design with scrollwork at top and bottom represent fine examples of turn-of-the-century wood baskets. Used for holding kindling during the pre-1920 era, these baskets are now finding wide use as magazine holders.

a synthetic material treated with glue and sometimes wrapped around an inner-core of wire at stress points in the designs to ensure durability. Although most Mission- and Bar Harbor-style wicker of this period was made of reed and willow, many new and unconventional designs combined two and sometimes three materials to satisfy the esthetic demands of a particular design.

In keeping with its unique tradition, wicker furniture seemed to all but pass over the Art Nouveau style that spanned the 1890s-to-1910 era. Manufacturers were not reluctant to adapt wicker to the new flowing, wavelike designs, but they found it nearly impossible to produce Art Nouveau pieces that could be identified as such and not linked with the recently rejected ornate Victorian

1910 wicker desk with center drawer
d built-in reed letter holders is
nked by a waste paper basket and
agazine rack from the early 1900s.

designs. It's a pity that the Art Nouveau style was stifled in the wicker world, for some truly beautiful designs might have evolved if only the public would have accepted them. However, flowing lines had become so objectionable that a writer in *The Art World* magazine commented wryly: "The other day I picked up a catalogue of willow furniture dated 1895. Nothing could be more horribly ornate, more foolishly cluttered with meaningless scrolls and excrescences. We have advanced a long way since that time."*

Early in the century some American manufacturers followed the Austrian penchant for upholstering wicker furniture, and by 1910 many armchairs, rockers, settees, and chaises longues sported luxurious cushions. Filled with horsehair or cotton, the cushions served a dual purpose: added comfort and a wider selection of covering using cretonne, tapestry, leather, chintz, and linen that could complement any given decor. The new wicker interior decorating concept was mentioned in *Country Life in America* in 1914: "the rapidly growing popularity of wicker is easily accounted for by the fact that the public has come to consider it as a legitimate article of interior decoration rather than a makeshift for porch and lawn use during the summer seasons. . . ."†

Suddenly, that subtle quality called "atmosphere" was on the mind of wicker consumers, and the correct combinations of design, finish, material, and pattern were of the utmost importance. From the type of stain to the cushion fabric used, color schemes were now a major factor in decorating with wicker. Gustav Stickley's magazine *The Craftsman* claimed that some people simply preferred "a different shade—a soft dull blue, a delicate gray or mahogany to harmonize with the color scheme of drawing room, club room, bedroom or boudoir. . . . It is a charming fashion to have bedroom chairs of willow upholstered in chintz or cretonne to match the

---

*Walter A. Dyer, "A Justification of Wicker," *The Art World* (April 1917), p. 81.
†James Collier Marshall, "Among the Wicker Shops," *Country Life in America* (May 1914), p. 16.

Although the rolled serpentine arms and back of this settee are associated with the Victorian era, many early 1900s pieces employed the same design. Here the combination of a closely woven body and a contrasting open lower-back design of curlicues lightens the overall appearance of the piece.

This rare blanket chest was made around 1910 and placed at the foot of a bed for easy access. The closely woven angular design is highlighted by woven diamond patterns on the front and sides.

Handmade matching armchairs and ottoman from the turn of the century are indicative of the transitional period from Victorian to Mission style. Although the armchairs are considered a set, one chair is slightly larger than the other— the larger chair for a gentleman, the smaller chair for a lady.

window draperies, or to carry out the color scheme in rugs and wall."

Innovative Styles Cater to the Public

After 1910 major stylistic trends took a back seat to experimental designs emphasizing the individual qualities of wicker pieces. Practical adaptations such as armchairs and rockers with woven side pockets under the arms were designed as handy receptacles for magazines and knitting supplies. On the other hand, impractical innovations were introduced with limited success and vanished quickly from the scene. Witness the "Rubber Cushion Rocker" patented by the Puritan Company of Gardner, Massachusetts, which shod the bottom of wooden rockers with "rubber tires" claiming it "a boon to nervous people and indispensable to initiated lovers of luxury."

The success rate of new designs far outweighed the number of frivolous ideas rejected by the public. Oil lamps with woven willow bases and shades were replaced by electric lamps of increasingly sophisticated designs in both floor and table models. Wicker porch or veranda furniture was being designed in a rustic mode with turned pine or "old hickory" framework and closely woven reed or willow panels. Some porch furniture was so specialized that circular refreshment holders were built into the arms of chairs and lounges.

Wicker baby carriages underwent significant changes. Major manufacturers offered "Pullman Sleeper Coaches" with fancy parasols and plush interiors, "Park Carts" without tops, two-wheeled "Sulkies" pulled along with handles, and the ever-popular "Go-Carts." The latter carriage was a semi-collapsible design developed by the Block Go-Cart Company of Philadelphia. The crowning touch in pre-1920 carriages came with the 1916 Heywood Brothers and Wakefield Company miniature version of a Ford automobile, complete with ball-bearing wheels, rubber tires, license plate, windshield, nickle-plated hub caps, and corduroy upholstery.

No study of turn-of-the-century wicker would be complete without mention of the industry's supreme achievement: the development and perfection of exquisitely made wicker phonograph cabinets. By 1915 the demand for unique, high-quality phonographs resulted in the manufacture of "Perfek'tone" wicker phonograph cabinets by the Heywood Brothers and Wakefield Company. With the emphasis falling on cabinetry and styling, these odd-

The understated jardinière planter complements the closely woven, conservative design of this popular Mission-style settee.

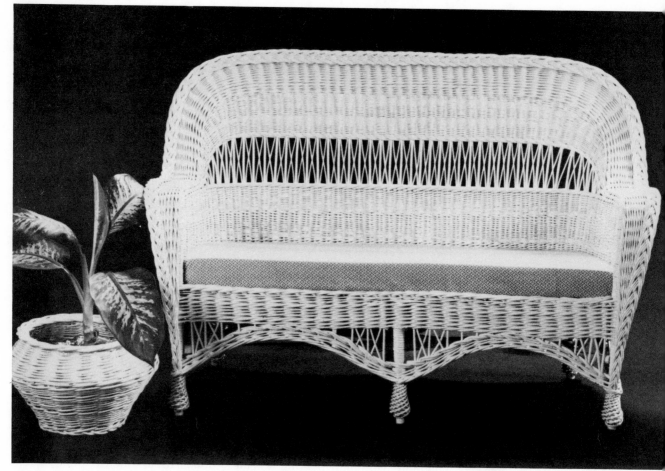

looking phonographs were advertised as the most advanced music machines. The reed-and-cane-wrapped cabinets were said to eliminate the annoying "countervibrations" so noticeable in conventional wood cabinets. With both floor and table models available, as well as a choice of hand-crank and electrically driven triple spring motor varieties, the consumer was further snowed with advertisements such as the following in 1919:

> The Perfek'tone Reproducer is made to match with scientific exactness the perfect construction of the human organs of sound.
>
> The effect of the Perfek'tone Reproducer is such that even the untrained ear can appreciate the purity of tone. The elimination of all metallic and mechanical sounds means that the greatest barrier to the successful reproduction of sound has been overcome.
>
> The Horn, or tone amplifier, is of special design and construction. It is composed of a matrix of wood and fabric having a peculiarly vibratory action of its own, and gives a fullness and sweetness of tone which can be compared to a rare old violin. Violins made of this material reproduce the tones of very old and seasoned wood.
>
> The Perfek'tone Cabinet is the last word in acoustical science as applied to sound-reproducing instruments, having no confined air spaces or cavities to destroy the original coloring of the music. The counter vibrations, so noticeable with wood cabinets, are entirely eliminated by the use of reed and cane.
>
> These three things control the perfect reproduction of the music. They are contained in all Perfek'tone instruments, making the quality and tone of the music the same, irrespective of the size and shape of the cabinet.

6

WHEN THE MACHINE AGE CAME ALONG

The Lloyd Loom

During World War I, severe economic conditions caused a tremendous increase in import duties on rattan. After an unsuccessful attempt by the Department of Agriculture to create a domestic willow-raising industry, it became clear that economic uncertainties (rather than a public shift in taste) would determine the type of wicker furniture that would be on the market. Although closely woven wicker made from reed was economically unfeasible, it was what the public wanted. To fill this need a synthetic material called "fiber" (already mentioned in Chapter 4) came into greater use. This inexpensive, chemically treated kraft paper, made from wood pulp, was twisted into tight rolls that were stiffened with glue to ensure the shape of each design. Wicker manufacturers increased their use of this material with closely woven wicker furniture to offset the high labor costs of workers using reed. In 1912 only 15 percent of all wicker furniture was made of fiber, but by 1920 that figure jumped to nearly 50 percent and then beyond.

This very rare buffet-server from the 1920s stands five feet in height and includes four glass-paneled cupboards, three silverware drawers, and two spacious storage doors below.

77

This magazine advertisement from Lloyd Manufacturing Company in 1907 features popular wicker teddy bear vehicles that are rare finds today.

Above right: This hard-to-find early 1920s wicker buffet has a large top, three silverware drawers, storage shelves, and a center compartment.

Below right: The back of this large eight-legged office desk exhibits the popular 1920s woven diamond pattern. Five drawers and woven bookshelves on the opposite side offer ample storage space.

In April of 1917, the very month that America entered "the war to end all wars," Walter A. Dyer wrote about the state of the wicker industry in an article, "A Justification of Wicker"; he claimed that reed or willow could be "woven upon a framework in close or open mesh which gives an opportunity for a wide variety of decorative effects. The result is a strong, durable piece of furniture, light to move about, elastic and unequaled for comfort, with a surface which is not easily marred or scratched and that may be cleaned with a damp cloth. The necessity for handwork keeps it out of the cheap class of furniture, and yet the average prices are moderate."

At the time Dyer was writing about the "necessity for handwork," Marshall B. Lloyd of Menominee, Michigan, patented his

Collectible wicker from the 1920 era
dominates this sunroom. Every piece is
handmade of reed except the two inner-
spring fiber rockers.

revolutionary "Lloyd loom." Suddenly mechanization hit the wicker
furniture industry. Utilizing fiber, Lloyd invented the loom at his
factory, the Lloyd Manufacturing Company (established in 1906),
which specialized in the making of wicker baby buggies and go-
carts. In the Heywood-Wakefield Company centennial publication,
A Completed Century, we are told of the unique circumstances
under which the development of the loom took place:

> One of the most expensive processes in the manufacture of these
> carriages had always been the weaving of the wicker bodies,
> since weaving a body by hand required an entire day, however
> expert the weaver. The efforts to construct a loom capable of
> weaving fibre were accelerated in 1917, when a strike occurred
> among the reed workers at the Lloyd plant. Mr. Lloyd acceded
> in part to most unreasonable demands, but with the assent went

the warning that the time was at hand when such demands would defeat their own purpose. The men were still dissatisfied, and finally the plant was closed down for five weeks. During that period Mr. Lloyd worked night and day on the new looms, and when the factory reopened many workmen found that their services were no longer needed. A strange new machine capable of performing the work of thirty men had taken the place of many a worker. This invention of Mr. Lloyd's changed a small organization into one of the largest baby-carriage factories in the world."*

The "strange new machine" was a circular loom that operated in a rotary manner, weaving fiber in an over-and-under manner to form flat sheets of wickerwork. Lloyd had succeeded where so many other inventors had failed because he had a new concept in

*A Completed Century, 1826–1926: The Story of Heywood-Wakefield Company (Boston: Updike, 1926), p. 38.

stylish 1920s telephone chair with an
k side table sports a decorative
angular reed design.

An early 1920s arched double planter is combined with a hanging birdcage and aquarium.

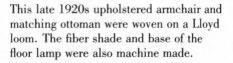

This late 1920s upholstered armchair and matching ottoman were woven on a Lloyd loom. The fiber shade and base of the floor lamp were also machine made.

overall construction. Rather than trying to develop a machine that would weave fiber over a frame, he made a loom that wove the wickerwork separately; when the process was completed the wicker "fabric" was carefully fitted over preassembled frames. The editor of *Scientific American* magazine was so impressed that he wrote in a 1920 article:

> Century after century has found this ancient art [weaving] handed down and down and down without development. Many tried to improve it and failed, until it became an accepted fact that the method of producing wicker goods was a supreme gift to mankind and that no improvements were possible. Today it is being improved.*

By lowering the cost of labor and expensive imported materials, Marshall B. Lloyd quickly became the largest manufacturer of wicker baby buggies in the country and subsequently branched out into machine-made wicker furniture. The public had yearned for inexpensive closely woven wicker since 1910. Lloyd knew that he could fulfill that wish by mass-producing "Lloyd loom" furniture. In no time, the Lloyd Manufacturing Company was a powerful force in the wicker industry.

The Heywood-Wakefield Company

In February of 1921 the Heywood Brothers and Wakefield Company bought out the Lloyd Manufacturing Company and the Lloyd loom patent. To mark the occasion the official corporate title was simplified to the Heywood-Wakefield Company. It was a wise move on the part of shrewd executives; the ever-increasing price of rattan and rising craftsmen's wages had made it clear that hand-woven wicker furniture made with natural materials could not compete with machine-woven wicker made with synthetic material. Thus

---

*George W. Rowell, Jr., "How a Manual Art of Five Thousand Years Standing Has Succumbed to Mechanical Methods," *Scientific American* (March 6, 1920), p. 242.

the newly titled Heywood-Wakefield Company made Marshall B. Lloyd a director as well as manager of the Menominee factory. At this time, the three main factories divided responsibilities. The Gardner factory housed the lumber yard, designing department, wood shop, carriage department, and chemical laboratory. The Wakefield factory housed the cane-weaving machinery, car-seating department, and matting department. And the seventeen-acre Menominee factory housed the fiber-spinning department (including a figure-eight braiding machine and a shaped fabric loom), metal-working department, weaving room, and upholstery department.

While the 1920s were dominated by machine-made wicker, some fine handmade pieces were produced. However, the Lloyd loom had such a profound effect on public taste that even handmade wicker designs were strongly influenced by machine designs. The public liked the uniformity of the machine-made weave as well as the rational construction of these pieces. Yet there were still some important innovations in designs during the twenties that advanced the state of the art. Designers continued to perfect phonograph cabinets. Wicker library tables became extremely popular in homes, in hallways and parlors. The sofa or davenport all but replaced the settee. Capable of seating three or four people comfortably, sofas ranged from sixty to eighty-five inches in length and usually came with springs attached to the framework or contoured inner-spring cushions. There was also the "Lomodi," the predecessor of today's "hide-a-bed." Wicker infiltrated kitchens with the introduction of buffets and china cabinets, while greater numbers of tea carts, smoking stands, coat racks, tables, and porch swings filled homes. The market was also flooded by a multitude of wicker lamp designs—some emphasizing "Eiffel tower"–type bases, others concentrating on intricately woven shades with silk lining. Complete dining sets, dressers, and dressing screens appeared everywhere. Wicker radio cabinets (with matching wicker speakers), extremely rare today, were also made during the twenties.

Open crisscross Bar Harbor weave (above and below the drawers) distinguishes this three-drawer natural buffet with solid oak shelves.

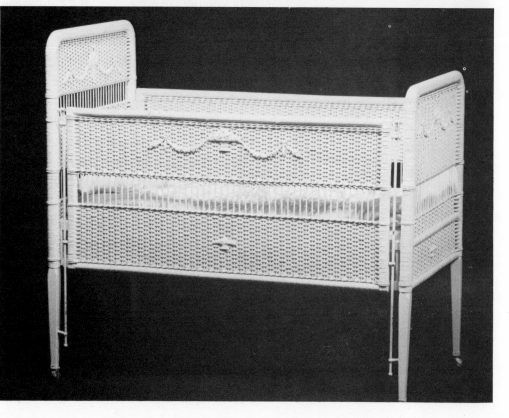

This sturdy crib from the mid-20s is handmade of closely woven reed. A gessoed flower design (made of molded plaster of Paris) adorns headboard, footboard, and side panels.

Again wicker ventured outside the home with the advent of custom-designed wicker stools with low backs for lunch counters.

Aside from some notably innovative designs, the twenties saw the widespread use and acceptance of such money-saving practices as using turned wood framework that at first glance looked like wrapped cane. Gessoed roses and molded fancywork such as flower wreaths made of plaster of Paris became popular during this decade. More than ever before wicker manufacturers increased their use of inexpensive materials such as Oriental sea grass and prairie grass. Both materials were hand-twisted and displayed a variegated green and tan color. Unlike fiber, Oriental sea grass and prairie grass were not adaptable to a mechanical loom and dictated hand weaving.

Factory-painted wicker furniture was also on the rise after World War I. Bright, eye-catching shades of green and red were very popular, as were specialty colors, such as Ming blue, canary yellow, and turquoise. Of course, the old standards—white, forest green, and black—remained the favorites. A completely new painting method was also introduced during this period: the "Duo-Tone Enamel Finish." First, an undercoat and enamel of the same color were applied and allowed to dry. Then came a "toner" of a contrasting yet complementary color. Before the toner dried it was wiped off lightly with a cloth so as to leave it between the strands of wicker-work. This way, the higher surfaces of the weave were wiped dry to expose the original enamel; hence the term "duo-tone."

Beyond the introduction of the Lloyd loom, the biggest change in twenties wicker furniture was the increased dependence on upholstery. Wicker relied heavily on padded cushion backs as well as cushioned and inner-spring seats. Many of the backs on armchairs, rockers and sofas were partially upholstered, using cretonne in blues, greens, and browns. If the pieces were left in

This rare and valuable four-drawer dresser from the mid-192•
has an adjustable mirror that reflects the triangular pattern •
top.

Above: A single-drawer desk set of fiber employs an uncommon flowing design from the 1920s.

Above right: A handmade lamp from the mid-1920s rests atop a machine-made oval table with glass top and closely woven base.

their natural state or painted in soft colors, the seats and cotton-filled backrests were often covered with brightly colored prints.

Competitors

Although popular wicker imports—Hong Kong's hourglass chair, the Philippines' peacock, and French enameled cane furniture—remained on the market, the vast quantity of fine wicker furniture was still made in America. While older established manufacturers like Schober and Company (established in 1892) added Far East imports to their line for diversification, new companies sponsored a revival in quality hand-crafted wicker and experimental designs. Although established in 1878, Joseph P. McHugh & Company came into its own during the twenties with highly unconventional designs featuring reed and willow that gave the Heywood-Wakefield Company some serious competition. Other competitors cropped up after World War I: Art Rattan Works in California, Grand Rapids Fiber Cord Company in Michigan, and High Point Bending and Chair Company in Silver City, North Carolina; the Kaltex Furniture Company of Jackson, Michigan; the Madison Basketcraft Company of Burlington, Iowa; the Midland Chair and Seating Company of Michigan City, Indiana; the Prairie Grass Furniture Company of Long Island, New York; Reedfibre of Ionia, Michigan; the Bemis Riddell Fibre Company of Sheboygan, Wisconsin; the Wicker-Kraft Company of Newburgh, New York; Willow & Reed of Brooklyn, New York; and the Ypsilanti Reed Furniture Company of Ionia, Michigan; to name a few.

The Beginning of the End

The mid-1920s witnessed a shift toward Art Deco. Named for an exhibition held in Paris in 1925, "L'esposition Intérnational des Arts Décoratives," the Art Deco designs in wicker furniture were based on rational construction, simple ornamentation, and geometric lines. Striving for harmony and balance of design, wicker manufacturers began producing pieces with conservative curving lines that were dictated by proportion and good taste. As for fancywork, there was the ubiquitous diamond pattern woven into backs of chairs and settees, but even it was a controlled geometric design added for balance rather than artistic whim. Diamond patterns were often painted a different and sometimes contrasting color at the factory to produce a strong visual impact and three-dimensional quality. Art Deco wicker had its day, but it was a short-lived phenomenon and the last major style used by the American wicker furniture industry.

Late in the twenties wicker began to loose its grip on the American public. Disenchanted wicker buyers turned their backs

An upholstered fiber rocker from the early 1920s boasts a diamond pattern back rest that is offset by an unusual teardrop design beneath the arms.

on machine-made, mass-produced pieces, longing for the uniquely individual feel wicker once possessed. It went the way of the machine, helped along by Art Deco. The sterile uniformity of design and the inferior quality of materials like fiber were rejected by the public. By 1927 wicker manufacturers realized that the entire industry was in deep trouble but did not know what to do. They tried elaborate advertising campaigns in magazines and new styles, such as "stick wicker" emphasizing vertical lines, but nothing seemed to work. Blindly, they made wicker pieces by hand that were designed with a "modern" machine-made look. Had they been more attuned to the art of handmade wicker furniture and not merely to sales figures, they might have realized that the public had come full circle. Innovative as it was, the Lloyd loom was

Above: These classic machine-made wicker pieces from the late 1920s were woven on a Lloyd loom and manufactured by the Heywood-Wakefield Company.

Below: This closely woven fiber couch was made in the late 1920s on a Lloyd loom.

Serpentine-backed settee from the 1890s displays scrollwork, wooden beadwork, and the period's ever-present curlicues.

dismissed as just another labor-saving contraption. Machine-made wicker was drawing its last breath.

The American wicker industry had lost touch with its roots. Continued use of heavy upholstery proved that the manufacturers simply didn't understand the problem. Originally the most popular aspect of wicker furniture had always been its elasticity and ability to give with the weight of its user. If construction had been kept on a high level of craftsmanship, the magic of wicker might have continued hypnotizing future generations. However, it was not meant to be. The early thirties witnessed the death of a once thriving industry, as well as a totally unique, functional art form.

❧ 7 ❧

WICKER WAS THERE

Wicker furniture was so adaptable and popular with the American public between 1885 and 1925 that it was found almost everywhere. Aside from being used in every room in the house, it was used on porches, in gazebos, and in summer gardens.

Away from the home, wicker had a strong link with transportation. Beyond pony carts, elaborate sulkies, and closely woven street car seats, wicker was used as railroad seating in everything from mahogany-paneled private cars to smoking and observation lounges. Many trains that used wicker were special "excursion trains" intended to meet the tourists' needs as they journeyed between the great watering places and resorts of the day.

Wicker went aboard boats, ships, and airplanes, too. Because of its lightness and immunity from dampness, wicker was pressed into use on every seaworthy vessel imaginable—from custom row-boat seats to sturdy armchairs on private yachts. Wicker was even put to use in the form of seats in the early passenger airplanes of the 1920s because of its lightness.

Regardless how the weary traveler reached his destination, he was met by wicker furniture in the grand lobbies of resorts. Wicker made its way into sun rooms, garden rooms, ladies' parlors, and meandering porches of these luxurious spas as well. Wicker seemed to be everywhere.

This turn-of-the-century father proudly stands alongside his child, who seems quite comfortable in a plushly upholstered and parasol-covered, semi-collapsible baby carriage, or "go-cart."

General and Mrs. John B. Gordon used Victorian wicker throughout their palatial Atlanta home, as shown in this mid-1890s photograph, with notable pieces like the conversation chair in the center of the room, the settee directly behind it, and the Turkish chair at right.

lark Gable and Vivien Leigh in the 1939 movie
one with the Wind push their daughter down
e streets of Atlanta in a fancy three-wheeled
icker carriage complete with stuffed horse
nd reins.

Joseph Jefferson, one of America's premier actors from 1865
to 1903, is chauffeured around West Palm Beach in a wicker
"tricycle chair" by his valet. These unique and extremely rare
wicker pieces were also known as "Afro-mobiles" because of
their black drivers.

After 1900 photographers often went from house to house offering their services, which included photographing subjects
with various props such as wicker pony or goat carts. In this
1919 photograph taken in California, two young Swedish im-
migrants pose for the camera.

A cancer-plagued Ulysses S. Grant recounts his memoirs at Mt. McGregor, New York, in 1885. Outdoors in this comfortable wicker armchair he wrote the bulk of his memoirs, completing the work a mere four days before his death on July 23, 1885.

Author Mark Twain relaxes on an impressive wicker chaise longue or "reclining chair" at Tuxedo Park, New York, in 1907. The lounge is typical of the 1890s serpentine design, which is in demand on today's market.

An 1890s Pullman car interior boasts closely woven, horse-hair-padded wicker railroad seats (made on a loom invented in 1870 by William Houston of the Wakefield Rattan Company).

Parlor car No. 500 is the "pride of the fleet" at the Branford Trolley Museum in East Haven, Connecticut. The 1904 railroad car's interior displays the individual wicker pieces that were a staple of railroad seating.

The wicker-filled Café Parisien on board the *Titan* was the place to be for after-dinner dancing.

❧ 8 ❧
INVESTING IN WICKER

Within the last decade the practice of investing in antiques and collectibles as an inflation hedge has grown tremendously. Inflation has sponsored the antiques boom by providing an incentive to own things that don't produce current taxable income. Although "experts" consider art, antiques, and collectibles to be high risks, it doesn't take a financial wizard to realize that investing in classic cars, Tiffany glass, or bisque dolls in the 1960s would have been a wise and extremely profitable venture. As for the 1980s, antique wicker furniture may be the ticket. As a functional art form, wicker is finally coming into its own.

Specialization is the key word when investing in any antique. Since opinions on the authenticity, rarity, quality, and value of any antique vary from one expert to another, your best bet is picking one field and becoming your own expert.

Age should be one of the prime considerations when buying wicker furniture for investment. Generally speaking, any pre-1900 pieces are considered Victorian; these represent prospective investments because the Victorian period is considered the Golden Age of Wicker. Pieces from the early 1900s with definite styles,

This hard-to-find, hand-crank phonograph from the early 1920s is a fine investment piece.

such as Mission and Art Nouveau, can also be good investments. Even selected pieces from the 1920s can be effective hedges against inflation as long as they are rare, handmade, and in excellent condition. Forget about buying any machine-made wicker or post-1930 pieces with investment in mind. Here again, your education in the field is important; although dating a piece by style alone is never completely accurate, it should be used as one of the important bits of evidence.

An investor should do all that he or she can in establishing the approximate age of a piece. Since there are cases of popular designs that were introduced in the 1880s and, because of continued good sales, were still being made in the early 1900s, it's a good idea to search the piece for a company label. Although the majority of labels were paper and have disappeared with age, there are still those that have withstood the ravages of time. Aside from paper labels, there were metal and celluloid manufacturer's labels attached under the framework of the seat, to the back of the seat, or on one of the cross-braces under the seat on chairs, rockers, and settees. These can provide valuable leads in tracking down the era of a specific piece. The label will not only mention the company but also the factory location. Sometimes it is possible to do your own detective work through these labels by writing to the historical societies and museums in the manufacturer's town. Ask for information concerning the company, including its years of operation. Often a little research like this can produce some fascinating and well-documented results and, of course, add to the value of your investment.

Unless a specific year is stamped under the seat frame, it is impossible to accurately pinpoint the year of manufacture. However rare, thousands of pieces exist today with these often hard-to-locate stamped-in dates. They are desirable from a historical standpoint and definitely add to the value of a piece.

Regarding labels from the famous Heywood-Wakefield Company and its predecessors, any piece of wicker carrying a label with the Heywood or Wakefield name (or any combination thereof) should be given extra consideration in the investment field. These companies still carry the reputation of an entire industry. Since they had distinctive and clearly documented dates of operation, the following guidelines should help put any labeled piece into the correct time frame:

Wakefield Rattan Company	(1855–1897)
Heywood Brothers & Company	(1868–1897)
Heywood Brothers & Wakefield Company	(1897–1921)
Heywood-Wakefield Company	(1921)

Besides establishing the approximate manufacturing date, a label can greatly enhance the value of a piece of antique furniture by making the maker readily identified. With this in mind it's a good idea to protect any paper label from unnecessary heat or moisture.

his 1920s R.C.A. Radiola 18 parks the interest of collectors r two reasons: it is a pristine xample of early wooden radio abinetry coupled with a rare icker-covered speaker.

Wicker tea carts have always been a wise investment because of their rarity and their utility. This example from the early 1900s has a glass-topped removable serving tray and a spacious storage shelf below. A highly desirable lady's rocker from around 1870 is beside it. The loop design, the "star-back" caning pattern woven into the back panel, and the hand-caned seat are all important clues in accurately estimating the age of this piece.

Beside the obvious importance of age, an investment piece's overall condition is also of critical importance. The closer a piece comes to its original condition, the greater its value. Natural, or unpainted, wicker furniture is highly prized simply because there are fewer pieces available. You should also carefully check the piece in question for structural sturdiness. If it is wobbly and needs structural repair, keep in mind that usually some wickerwork must be removed to tighten a loose joint or make a repair. Then you're faced with finding a wicker restoration specialist capable not only of replacing the reed or cane but of matching the original stain. Much thought should be given to purchasing investment pieces in need of anything more than basic repair or perhaps new set-in or hand-caned seats. Even when examining a piece before purchase, you should always keep an eye out for noticeable repairs; an unprofessional restoration job can greatly diminish the value of a rare investment piece. When considering a rare but damaged piece of wicker, ask a professional wicker-restoration specialist to look at the piece and determine whether it can be restored properly.

Other factors to consider are the design, rarity, quality of materials, and overall craftsmanship of a given piece of wicker. Rare designs bring higher prices because of their scarcity. When you combine a rare design with a sturdy structure and good-quality reeds, you're well on your way to making an investment in antique wicker. Another goal to strive for is finding a piece in its original state. Regardless of whether it exhibits a deep mahogany stain, the "fancy-colored reeds" once popular in Victorian times, or the "duo-tone" paint jobs so much in evidence during the 1920s, the original finish is most desirable.

No matter how old or rare a piece, wicker should not be treated like gold bars and locked away in a vault. The beauty of wicker furniture is that it is both a work of art and a functional object. Part of the pleasure of investing in an exceptional piece of wicker is that it can be used and admired daily. Whether your decor is exotic or rustic in design, try incorporating investment pieces. Mixing distinctive antiques in an eclectic manner can add warmth and individuality to any home. Fine wicker furniture still possesses the charm it once had in winning the hearts of a younger America.

Truly rare pieces of wicker furniture are expected to appreciate sharply over the next decade. Investing in matching sets (such as a settee, chaise longue, armchair, and rocker of the same design and finish) is wise. Likewise, buying unique designs, such as Victorian "theme" chairs or rockers with woven back panels of sailboats, stars, bells, or banjos, has proved to be a good investment. Rare individual Victorian pieces worthy of consideration include conversation chairs, platform rockers, étagères, corner chairs, Morris chairs, piano chairs, music stands, chaises longues, picture frames, and easels. Handmade pieces from just after the turn of the century, such as phonograph cabinets, bookcases, halltrees, table and floor lamps, porch swings, dining sets, tea carts, grandfather clocks, vanities, china cabinets, electric fountains, and buffets, are usually sound investments, provided they are in very good to mint condition.

Just as there are characteristics to look for when buying wicker, there are things to avoid. After you develop an eye for handmade wicker, it will be easy for you to spot machine-made pieces. Stay away from machine-made furniture or other pieces made with fiber, even if they were handmade. Fiber often unwraps from its tightly twisted roll and, even under layers of paint, is unattractive. Once unraveled, fiber tends to peel away or become fibrous. Practically all fiber and Oriental sea grass pieces were made after 1900, primarily in the twenties. Only extremely rare fiber or sea grass pieces are worthwhile to investors.

Beware of heavily painted pieces, "marriages" (for example, a replaced, mismatched lampshade), and reproductions. Detecting a reproduction is a common problem for beginners. If you suspect that a piece is a reproduction, test its weight in relation to other wicker pieces you know to be antique. The imported reproductions, made with rattan or bamboo framework, are much lighter than their antique counterparts, which used hardwood framework. Another sure sign of a reproduction is the use of circular reed seating employing the under-and-over weave. These poorly designed seats are often the first thing to be damaged on a cheap reproduction chair or settee because they are not adequately secured to the framework. Keep in mind that the great majority of antique wicker chairs used either cane seats or horizontally woven seats of round reed that were wrapped around the framework. Also keep a suspicious eye out for pieces with an overabundance of curlicues set

A true museum piece, this armchair converts into a lounge
Chairs like this (produced on a very limited basis during 1870
1885) offer one of the best investments on the market.

into the back or under the arms and legs, the telltale shine of new brass-plated caps on the feet, and poor-quality reed and cane, which is often very fibrous and dry looking. In fact, the very best way to protect yourself against buying reproductions is to do a little leg work. Visit some import shops that carry new wicker furniture. You'll soon see that it doesn't take an expert to tell the difference between a fraud and the real thing.

Finding quality antique wicker is getting harder all the time. Geographically the eastern, midwestern, and northern states have more wicker to choose from since most of the large companies were located there, but it's available practically everywhere, in varying degrees. The growth of antique wicker specialty shops in the 1970s was very dramatic, and today these shops are probably the best source for finding rare wicker worthy of serious investment. Not only do the shopowners carry a large selection of fine wicker furniture, but they offer an invaluable source of information. As specialists in the field, these dealers can usually answer difficult questions about wicker and provide information concerning the rarity, style, and value of a given piece. Most dealers are also wicker-restoration specialists themselves or can put you in touch with the people who do their wicker repairs. Their expertise enables them to obtain the finest-quality pieces available from across the country.

Antique shows and flea markets provide some very good investment pieces, but, again, be advised that the best way of protecting yourself from overpriced wicker or reproductions is to know your wicker furniture. Once armed with a wide knowledge of your specialization, you can actually be one up on "weekend dealers" at flea markets or garage sales. It's possible to make some incredible deals with a little luck. While antique shows usually carry higher-quality merchandise than flea markets, the dealers are often shopowners and therefore knowledgeable about prices. Regardless, these shows (as well as flea markets) are a good place to meet

Right: The flowing lines of these three pieces—an 1880s table, a 1915 lamp, and an 1890s armchair—complement each other, regardless of the fact that they represent different periods of wicker design.

Below: Not only is this 1860s couch considered a very early wicker piece, but the design is extremely rare and desirable because full-length couches were seldom made before the 1890s.

people with a similar interest, and there is usually an exchange of ideas, sources, and specific facts concerning the wicker for sale. One word of caution if you plan to attend a mid- to large-sized flea market: expect some aggressive competition from collectors as well as from dealers. The early riser can usually come across some deals. If you know that a piece of wicker is worth the asking price, don't say, "I'll think about it." Chances are, someone else right behind you is doing a little thinking of his own, such as how he can fit it into his car after buying it. "Fleas" (as they are affectionately known) have always been an aggressive game, but they've become even more so perhaps over the past few years with the unprecedented collecting boom of the 1970s. A newcomer to the famous Brimfield flea market in Massachusetts might well think

Wicker conversation chairs have always been good investments. This particular chair, manufactured around 1890, makes use of dual set-in cane seats, birdcage designs under the arms, curlicues, wooden beadwork, circular scrollwork, and closely woven yet intricately patterned back rests.

he's fallen down the rabbit hole in *Alice's Adventures in Wonderland*, what with predawn buyers running from one booth to the next with a flashlight in one hand and a walkie-talkie in the other. It's first come, first served at these tea parties!

Antique auctions can turn up some quality wicker, but they can also be dangerous for the novice if he or she fails to carefully inspect the merchandise beforehand. Don't engage in random buying or get carried away in the heat of the moment and fail to stick to a predetermined bidding limit. Sit in on a few auctions before jumping in headfirst. They can teach the collector quite a bit about current prices and availability. Once you have attended an auction or two you will probably want to join in the bidding yourself. As a prospective buyer, first you should thoroughly examine the wicker

Furniture that sports motifs such as fans, stars, or hearts (known as "theme" pieces) are popular with collectors. These star-back and heart-back rockers from the 1880s are no exception.

Because of limited production, this 1880s decorative firescreen with tapestry panel is an extremely rare wicker item.

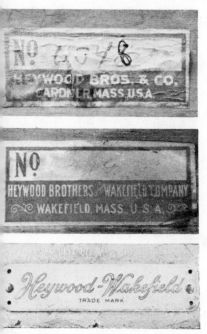

e of the only substantial clues to the
 of an antique wicker piece is a
nufacturer's label. Most often found
ner under the seat frame or at the
k of the seat frame, this valuable
torical record greatly enhances the
ue of a given piece and should be
efully preserved. A "Heywood
thers & Company" paper label
firms that a piece was made during
 Victorian era. A red and white
eywood Brothers and Wakefield
mpany" label attests that a piece was
nufactured between 1897 and 1921.
lluloid labels with the "Heywood-
kefield" identification appear on
niture manufactured in 1921 or after.

you are interested in at the presale exhibition or preview. Inspect
the piece with a cool, logical eye and search for any labels, damage
to the wickerwork, structural weakness, or poorly repaired areas.
The presale inspection is an important step when considering the
rarity and condition of a possible investment piece. After weighing
all aspects, sit down and make a calm decision as to what the
piece is actually worth to you. Write down the price and stick to
it regardless of how hot the bidding becomes. Auctioneers realize
that emotion, not logic, takes over at an auction. No matter how
much thought went into your preauction limit, there is a spirit of
competition underlying all auctions. It's easy to get carried away
in your bidding during the fast-paced excitement. A well-known
rule of thumb concerning auction prices suggests that you should
pay a little less than the retail price range found in antique shops.
So keep a close eye on the current market prices for antique wicker
during your preauction research.

The real key to investing in antique wicker is education. Know
a good deal when you come across one; learn how to spot a reproduction; know what type of material went into the making of a
particular piece; and learn how to tell the sometimes subtle dif-
ferences in design and styles from various eras. Most importantly,
learn what is rare and considered desirable by wicker experts and
other investors. Moreover, talk to other collectors, dealers, and
restoration specialists about antique wicker furniture. Let it be
known that you are a collector and that you're searching for specific
pieces. Read books, magazines, and newspapers on antiques. Visit
antique shops regularly to keep abreast of current price ranges
and attend antique shows, auctions, and flea markets. Learn everything you can about antique wicker furniture; then start investing
with an eye toward the future.

❧ 9 ❧

REPAIRING AND CARING FOR WICKER

While wicker-furniture restoration was considered a lost art a mere decade ago, now a genuine revival exists in this highly specialized field. Today there are scores of dedicated professional wicker repair people across the country, capable of bringing virtual "basket cases" back to life. Yet not all repairs demand an expert's attention. Basic repair jobs can be carried out successfully by the layman, provided he or she follows instructions carefully and purchases the correct repair materials.

For the layman or the professional, patience is a prerequisite. A bit of the perfectionist's temperament goes a long way in completing even minor repair jobs. If you're in a hurry and want quick results, take your piece to a professional; a hasty repair job, however simple, may end up at his or her shop anyway. Likewise, for more difficult repairs than the basic techniques illustrated in the following pages, call a wicker restoration specialist (see Appendix I). These artisans are true pioneers in the wicker renaissance

professional wicker repairman
rebuilding the serpentine roll on the
back of a Victorian baby carriage.

121

and take great pride in their work. Years of experience have given many of these talented people a sixth sense as far as developing a feel for bringing back the original design. They can work wonders on wicker that most people judge ready for the dump. Regardless of whether it's a bothersome structural problem, the rebuilding of an entire rolled or "serpentine" arm, an extensive reweaving job, or the replacing of a missing curlicue design, the experienced wicker repair person can be a tremendous value to collectors, investors, and antiques dealers.

If you decide to try your own hand at basic wicker repair, first identify and purchase the correct type of material. Matching the original material or materials is not difficult, even though antique wicker often employed two and three different types of material. The five most common materials used in wicker furniture were reed (in both round and flat forms), binder cane, willow, Oriental sea grass, and fiber. To determine the type of material, cut off a short piece from the damaged area and take it to a large craft-supply shop to obtain a match, or send the sample to one of the mail-order wicker-supply houses listed in Appendix II. Supply houses can establish the type of material and explain how it can be ordered through their catalogues. Many of these companies ship their supplies via United Parcel Service, allowing a package to reach you within three to five days after payment is received.

While the professional wicker repair person makes use of specialized awls, electric drills, nail drivers, and viselike curlicue machines, the amateur need only be concerned with the following basic tools and related supplies:

Hammer
Sharp hand clippers or heavy scissors
Needle-nose pliers
White glue (Weldwood or Lepages recommended)
½-inch to ¾-inch wire nails with heads
An accurate match in both type and size of materials

Basic Repairs

Before using certain wicker materials, you must submerge them in water. Both round and flat reed must be soaked in water anywhere from ten to twenty minutes, depending on the thickness of the reed, in order to insure flexibility. Reed is extremely supple when wet but brittle when dry. It will snap easily if you try to use it without properly soaking it first. Soak only the portion that will be used for immediate repair. Otherwise the reed will fray, and it will develop a warped, waterlogged appearance if it is left to soak for more than thirty minutes.

Binder cane, the glossy-surfaced material used extensively in wrapping the framework of wicker furniture, should also be used while wet. Rather than completely submerging cane, it is better simply to pass it through water slowly before use, which lessens the chances of its snapping when wrapping framework. A word of caution about storing binder cane: keep it away from furnaces or other sources of excessive heat, for it will become brittle quickly.

No preparation is necessary for either Oriental sea grass or manmade fiber. They are very supple and can be worked dry from the coil.

The following basic repair techniques cover the three most common and easily remedied problems with damaged wicker furniture—unraveled cane, broken or missing "spokes," and unwoven reeds.

Wrapping with Binder Cane

The most common problem with damaged wicker is the unraveling of binder cane (wider than chair seat cane) from around a chair leg. Fortunately, it is also the easiest to solve. First, turn the chair upside-down so that the legs are sticking up for easy access. Next, unwrap the damaged or loose cane down the leg to a point where the existing cane is in good shape. Nail it securely on the inside of the leg so it will not unravel further. Then take a full length of

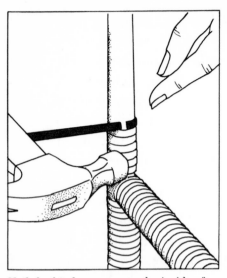

Nail the binder cane onto the inside of the chair leg where the old cane ends.

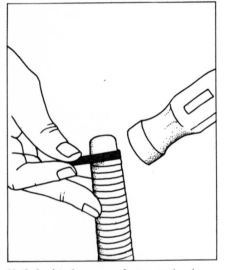

Nail the binder cane after wrapping is completed.

binder cane and, after passing it through water to insure suppleness, carefully nail it to the leg where the old cane ends (Illustration 1). To insure a permanent bond, run a thin bead of white glue up the leg to be wrapped. Then wind the cane slowly up the leg, taking care to wrap it tightly and evenly. When you come within half an inch of the leg end, nail the cane securely on the inside of the leg (Illustration 2) and snip off any excess. If your chair has metal foot caps at the end of the legs, wrap the cane all the way up to them before nailing the cane to the inside of the chair.

Replacing Broken Spokes

Most wicker furniture is composed of a skeleton of vertical reeds called "spokes." Replacing them is fairly simple. Before you begin this repair job, study the pattern that needs to be duplicated. On the majority of furniture the spokes are slanted in one direction at the front and in the opposite direction at the back.

First, remove the broken spoke two or three rows above the point where it enters the horizontal weave (Illustration 3). Repeat the same "snipping-out" process at the bottom of the spoke two or three rows below the beginning of the horizontal weave. Take a new presoaked reed and carefully cut it to size by inserting it into the top and bottom rows of the horizontal weave. When you obtain the correct bend in the spoke and it snaps tightly into both sections of the wickerwork, remove it. Place a generous amount of white glue on both ends of the new spoke. Now permanently set the bottom of the glued spoke into the weave. Bend the spoke in the middle so that it accurately follows the angle of the other spokes, and insert the glued tip into the top of the horizontal weave (Illustration 4). The new spoke should dry and stiffen into place so that it matches the other spokes. If you have trouble fitting the spoke into the weave, cut the ends of the reed at sharp angles so that the points fit through the horizontal weave without doing any damage. However, if you must cut these points, do it a bit at a

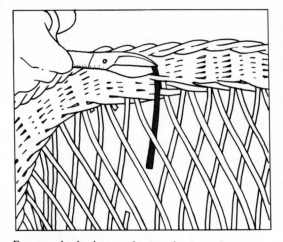

Remove the broken spoke in a horizontal weave with clippers.

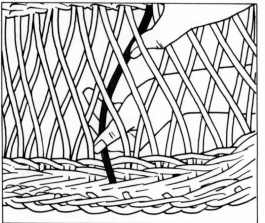

Insert the glued tip of the new spoke into the horizontal weave.

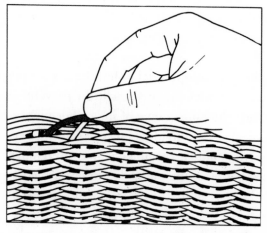

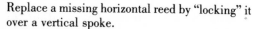

Replace a missing horizontal reed by "locking" it over a vertical spoke.

time while testing them for a tight fit. It is best to have as secure a fit as possible.

Locking Horizontal Reeds

Horizontal reeds that are woven alternately over and under vertical spokes sometimes need to be replaced. This calls for "locking," a patch-job method of laying together the ends of a weaving strand.

If a single horizontal reed is damaged, start your repair by clipping it off under the spokes directly to the left and right from the underside of the piece. When the horizontal reeds are clipped back flush under the spokes, a new length of presoaked reed should be cut and bent into place over the middle spoke and under the spokes to the left and right. It is best to place a bead of white glue at the top of the center spoke where the new reed will be placed. The fastening occurs when both ends of the new horizontal reed are "locked" under the freshly cut ends of the old reed (Illustration 5). When the replaced reed dries it tends to stiffen and therefore snap tighter against the bottom of the spokes to the left and right.

(Note: if the back or underside of the piece is not accessible, as in a hollow serpentine arm or back, slip a screwdriver under the damaged horizontal reed. Lift up sharply and snap it off behind the nearest vertical spoke.)

Tips on Cleaning Wicker

Although the care and upkeep of antique wicker furniture is simple enough, it is a wise collector who practices a little preventive medicine to further enhance the appearance of his or her pieces. Learn what materials make up each individual piece of your wicker. While a dusting brush attachment to a vacuum cleaner will remove dust from any furniture, other cleaning methods require a knowledge of wicker materials. For cleaning dirty wickerwork made of reed, cane, willow, or rattan a thorough going-over with a toothbrush and warm soapy water is recommended. However, usually all that is needed is a periodic wiping with a soft wet cloth or sponge. Don't worry that water will harm wicker made with these materials. Remember, rattan (and hence its byproducts, cane and reed) and willow are plants that thrive in swamplands. In fact, a simple outside sprinkling with a garden hose is the best remedy for bringing back wicker's natural elastic qualities whenever it seems dry or it creeks when in use. Water will feed these porous materials, ensuring continued flexibility. Badly soiled or discolored pieces made with these materials can be cleaned by dipping a toothbrush into a well-diluted mixture of domestic bleach. However, test this method first on the underside of your piece to make sure that results are satisfactory.

Wicker made of fiber or Oriental sea grass should not be subjected to water. Both of these materials should be cleaned only with a damp cloth. Remember, sometimes fiber (especially when heavily painted) can look like reed or willow, so carefully examine any material before using water. Hosing off a piece of wicker made of fiber could turn out to be a nightmare, since the tightly rolled kraft paper will become soggy and unravel.

Stripping Wicker

Because wicker porch furniture was often coated with paint every summer, the question of stripping wicker is often raised by the collector. It is a subject of heated debate among wicker specialists, dealers and collectors alike. Reed and willow pieces can be stripped to perfection or, conversely, all but ruined. Before making any decision, determine what materials were used in construction. Reed, rattan, cane, and willow can be stripped. Fiber and Oriental sea grass can be literally eaten away by chemicals. If you decide to strip a piece, find a professional furniture stripper or antiques-repair person who has successfully done the job before. Keep in mind that a stripper's chemical tank can raise small whiskerlike fibers on the reeds if the piece is left in too long. So make sure your wicker is left in as briefly as necessary to get 95 percent of the paint off. You can pick the stubborn chips away at home with an awl or an ice pick. After the paint has been removed, hose off the wicker outside, and let it dry for a few days before bringing it inside.

If you are leery of the stripper's hot-tank, you can hand strip a piece provided the intricacies of the design are not too elaborate.

For instance, many Bar Harbor pieces are made of thick reed in an open-weave design—perfect for stripping by hand. If you choose this somewhat tedious route, use a toothbrush and a high-quality water-soluble chemical remover. Again, at the risk of sounding overly cautious, I recommend turning the piece upside-down and doing a test patch in an inconspicuous area. It is worth the wait, since the results of different commercial paint removers vary widely.

Refinishing Natural Wicker

After cleaning or stripping, natural wicker can be left alone, but most people prefer to give it a coat of mineral oil, clear lacquer, clear varnish, or linseed oil for protection and a healthy sheen. You can produce a clear-finish solution by mixing the following ingredients:

⅓ linseed oil
⅓ McClosky Heirloom varnish
⅓ thinner

Another product, although hard to locate, is orange shellac. Made naturally by insects and pressed into sheets, this lightly honey-colored shellac is an excellent protective finish that allows the reeds to breathe and accept the necessary moisture for lasting elasticity.

An old practice from the early wicker factories, refinishing natural wicker pieces with stains is also very popular and attractive. Custom-stained pieces have always been a favorite with the public because a particular stain could be selected with a specific décor in mind. If you want to stain your wicker, first visit a good hardware or paint store to see the hues of various stains. Stains can be purchased in handy aerosol cans. Apply one light coat at a time to prevent drips, and allow one hour between coats if a slightly darker hue is desired.

Don't try staining a repair job to match an existing finish; that is best left to the professional wicker-restoration specialist or general antiques repairman. Nor should you try refinishing pieces that have already been stained or varnished. All stains or other finishes are not always compatible and may react unfavorably by blistering because of different chemical bases. It's best to leave these specialized areas to the experts.

Painting Wicker Furniture

Although natural wicker is of greater value to the serious collector and investor, painted pieces are far more prevalent on today's market. Many collectors like the painted look and feel it brightens up an otherwise drab room as no other type of furniture. But it is very unwise to paint a natural piece since there are so few around. There is enough painted antique wicker on the market to choose from without painting pieces in their original condition. However, if you wish to repaint a piece of wicker, the first step is to clean it thoroughly. If the paint is so heavy that it is flaking off, use a stiff brush to scrape all loose chips away from the piece and then hose it down. In some extreme cases the paint may be so thick that a quick dipping in a stripper's hot-tank is advisable. Remove three-quarters of the paint to start.

After preparing the piece you have three basic methods of painting to choose from:

1. Using a high-grade enamel paint in an aerosol can.
2. Using a specially prepared "wicker craft paint," available from many craft supply houses. This gloss white enamel comes in a can and must be applied with a brush, so the intricacies of the design may dictate whether or not you choose this method.
3. Using a high-grade acrylic enamel (combined with a reducing compound) and applying it with a compressor. A compressor produces the best results. The paint is applied more evenly, and the result is a professional-quality, long-lasting, durable coat.

Regardless of which method you use, remember that the best

results are always acquired by using oil-base paints. They are more durable and resist blistering when applied over previous coats of paint. Never use latex paint on wicker.

Before opening a can of paint, protect all manufacturer's labels on the wicker by carefully covering them with paper and masking tape. These are valuable historical records and add to the value of any piece. Then begin the actual painting process by turning the piece upside-down and painting the bottom first. When finished, turn it right side up and continue painting. Several thin coats applied at least one hour apart will result in a far better paint job than one heavy coat.

APPENDIXES

APPENDIX I
Wicker Restoration Specialists

ALABAMA

Allen's Antiques & Collectibles
121 Telegraph Road
Mobile, AL   36610

Mrs. Garnett Drake
Garnett's Wicker Shop
Route 6
Box 39
Decatur, AL   35603

ARKANSAS

Charlotte Thompson
1544 Crestwood
North Little Rock, AR   72116

ARIZONA

In Days of Old
2217 North 7th Street
Phoenix, AZ   85024

The Seat Weaving Shop
2214 North 24th Street
Phoenix, AZ   85024

CALIFORNIA

Agelong
1102 Hyde Street
San Francisco, CA   94109

Cane & Basket Supply Company
1283 South Cochran Avenue
Los Angeles, CA   90019

The Finishing Touch
5636 College Avenue
Oakland, CA   94618

The Hays House of Wicker
1730 East Walnut
Pasadena, CA   91106

Peter J. Isgrow
Isgrow & Company
1125 Soquel Avenue
Santa Cruz, CA   95062

Lightfoot House
8259 Melrose Avenue
Los Angeles, CA   90046

Tanglewood Furniture Restoration
325 Pennsylvania Avenue
Santa Cruz, CA   95062

Lew Tut
2615 South El Camino Real
San Mateo, CA   94401

Mike Bradbury
Windsor's Cane & Wicker Repair
130 East 17th Street
Suite G
Costa Mesa, CA   92627

CONNECTICUT

Paul's Furniture Repair Shop
23 First Street
East Norwalk, CT   06855

Henry Spieske
The Wicker Fixer
1052 Rear Main Street
Newington, CT   06111

Dick Alexander
Yesterday's Yankee
Lovers Lane
Lakeville, CT   06039

FLORIDA

Michael Calyore
5307 Shirley Street
Naples, FL   33942

Den of Antiquity
612 North Andrews Avenue
Ft. Lauderdale, FL   33311

Denis Beaver
The Key West Wicker Works
913 Duval Street
Key West, FL   33040

Gabriel Russo and Jim Swisher
Rosie's on Duval
901 Duval Street
Gingerbread Square
Key West, FL   33040

Von Wood Products
571 N.W. 71st Street
Miami, FL   33150

GEORGIA

Gail Dearing and Jeanne Barlow
Heirloom Wicker
Cates Center
110 E. Andrews Drive, N.W.
Atlanta, GA   30305

W. B. Lewis
231 Chatham Avenue
Pooler, GA   31322

Sheralyn's Antiques
1056 Murphy Avenue
Atlanta, GA   30310

ILLINOIS

Bill and Lee Stewart
The Collected Works
905 Ridge Road
Willmette, IL   60091

Kathy Olin
Route 1
Mt. Vernon, IL   62864

C. J. Lundgren
808 East Liberty
Wauconda, IL   60084

INDIANA

Vic and Anne Durkin
Antique Repair Shoppe
7222 Magoun Avenue
Hammond, IN   46324

Ron Rouser
The Yellow Wagon
400 West Melbourne
Logansport, IN   46947

IOWA

Belding's Furniture Restoration
2734 Mt. Vernon Road S.E.
Cedar Rapids, IA   52403

Kathy Glasgow
R.R. 1
Box 162
Danville, IA   52623

Wilson's Wicker & Weaving
1509 Main Street
Cedar Falls, IA   50613

LOUISIANA

The Wicker Gazebo
3137 Magazine Street
New Orleans, LA   70115

MAINE

Elizabeth and Richard King
Antique Wicker
Main Street
Northeast Harbor, ME   04662

MARYLAND

Len's Country Barn Antiques
9929 Rhode Island Avenue
College Park, MD   20740

Margaret Whippee
Whippee's Wicker
523 Herring Avenue
Fairhaven, MD   20754

Linda and Garry Koch
The Wicker Lady of Maryland
505 Jumpers Hole Road
Severna Park, MD   21146

MASSACHUSETTS

Jack L. Blake
7 Dr. Lord's Road
Dennis, MA   02638

Bostonia Furniture Company
183 Friend Street
Boston, MA   02114

Charlotte Wagner
The Wicker Lady
1197 Walnut Street
Newton Highlands, MA   02161

Frank H. McNamee
The Wicker Porch
Route 28
Cranberry Highway
Wareham, MA   02571

Marla Segal
Wicker Unlimited
P.O. Box 128
22 Skinner's Path
Marblehead, MA   09145

MINNESOTA

Theodore and Elaine Kvasnik
The Wicker Shop
2040 Marshall Avenue
St. Paul, MN   55104

Wicker West Repair Shop
174 West 7th Street
St. Paul, MN   55401

MISSOURI

Mary's
9615 Manchester
Rock Hill, MO   63119

Mike and Cheri Russel
The Wicker Fixer
Route 1
Box 283-B
Ozark, MO   65721

NEW JERSEY

Marcey Hedgepeth
Route 179
Ringoes, NJ   08551

Jones' Antiques
Oak Road & Harding Highway
Buena Acres, N.J.   08310

NEW YORK

Hazel and Neil Terwilliger
Buckboard Antiques
Box 129–08
Wallkill, NY   12589

Tony Karlovich
Cubbyhole Antiques
145 Main Street
Nyack, NY   10960

Mary Ellen Funk
P.O. Box 811
Quogue, NY   11959

Bernie Lowther
Rosycheeks
101 Atlantic Avenue
Brooklyn, NY   11206

Dottie and Ken Thomson
Round Lake Antiques
Box 358
Route 9
Round Lake, NY   12151

Pam Thompson
Wacky Wicker Worker II
P.O. Box 1
Constantia, NY   13044

Pat Steinbeiser
The Wicker Witch
6 Bradley Street
Marcellus, NY   13108

OHIO

Ohio Chair Company, Inc.
3447 West 130th Street
Cleveland, OH   44111

Howard Secrest
2976 Bishop
Cleveland, OH   44143

Jim and Marian Redmond
The Wacky Wicker Workers
Mentor, OH   44060

Judy Sikorski
Wickering Heights
411 Superior Street
Rossford, OH   43460

OKLAHOMA

Loren L. Lewis, Jr.
1228 North Yale
Tulsa, OK   74115

Nelson's Furniture Refinishing &
   Repair
1112 North Broadway
Oklahoma City, OK   73103

OREGON

Sue Kaady
14915 South Greentree Drive
Oregon City, OR   97045

Kathleen Lynch Caning, Rush &
   Wicker Repair
87867 Cedar Flat Road
Springfield, OR   97477

Donna Allison
The Wicker Workshop
115 West California Street
P.O. Box 584
Jacksonville, OR   97530

TEXAS

The Chair Repair Company
5807 Star
Houston, TX   77057

Garcia's Wicker & Rattan
   Refinishing
2817 West Davis
Dallas, TX   75211

The Old Wicker Garden
3111 Knox
Dallas, TX   75205

The Wicker Doctor
327 Summertime
San Antonio, TX   78216

Jane Davis
The Wicker Works
816 South Boure
Amarillo, TX   79102

VIRGINIA

Mr. and Mrs. William D. Critzer
773 Oyster Point Road
Newport News, VA   23602

Slim and Wanda Wilberger
Mr. Whisker's Attic
321 Airport Drive
Highland Springs, VA   23075

WASHINGTON

Alan Serebrin
Wicker Design Antiques
515 15th East
Seattle, WA   98112

The Wicker Works
15 Casino Road
Everett, WA   98204

WISCONSIN

Bea Niles
The Wickery
644 College Street
Milton, WI   53563

APPENDIX II
Wicker Supply Sources

CALIFORNIA

Cane & Basket Supply Company
1283 South Cochran Avenue
Los Angeles, CA   90019

Frank's Cane & Rush Supply
7244 Heil Avenue
Huntington Beach, CA   92647

T.I.E., Inc.
P.O. Box 1121
San Mateo, CA   94403

COLORADO

Loomcraft
Box 65
Littleton, CO   80160

Skyloom Fibres
1905 South Pearl
Denver, CO   80210

CONNECTICUT

Connecticut Cane & Reed Company
P.O. Box 1276
Manchester, CT   06040

The H. H. Perkins Company
10 South Bradley Road
Woodbridge, CT   06525

FLORIDA

Von Wood Products
571 N.W. 71st Street
Miami, FL   33150

GEORGIA

The Source
18 Peachtree Place
Box 7415
Atlanta, GA   30309

ILLINOIS

Bersted's
521 West 10th Avenue
Box 40
Monmouth, IL   61462

Dick Blick Company
P.O. Box 1267
Galesburg, IL   61401

MARYLAND

Macmillan Arts & Crafts
9645 Gerwig Lane
Columbia, MD   21046

MASSACHUSETTS

Bergan Arts & Crafts, Inc.
P.O. Box 381
Marblehead, MA   09145

The Whitaker Reed Company
90 May Street
Box 172
Worcester, MA   01602

MICHIGAN

Bexell & Son
2470 Dixie Highway
Pontiac, MI   48055

Delco Craft Center, Inc.
30081 Stephenson Highway
Madison Heights, MI   48071

MINNESOTA

Maid of Scandinavia Company
3244 Raleigh Avenue
Minneapolis, MN   55416

MISSOURI

WSI Distributors
1165 First Capital Drive
P.O. Box 1235
St. Charles, MO   63301

NEW HAMPSHIRE

New Hampshire Cane & Reed
   Company
65 Turnpike Street
Suncook, NH   03275

NEW JERSEY

Boin Arts & Crafts Company
87 Morris Street
Morristown, NJ   07960

Peerless Rattan & Reed
   Manufacturing Company
45 Indian Lane
Towaco, NJ   07082

NEW YORK

Albert Constantine & Son
2050 Eastchester Road
Bronx, NY   10461

Craftsman Supply House
35 Brown's Avenue
Scottsville, NY   14546

Eli Caning Shop
86 Wood Road
Centereach, NY   11702

NORTH CAROLINA

A'NL's Hobbycraft, Inc.
50 Broadway
P.O. Box 7025
Asheville, NC   28807

Billy Arthur, Inc.
University Mall
Chapel Hill, NC   27514

OHIO

Cane Shop
15635 Madison Avenue
Cleveland, OH   44107

Ohio Chair Company, Inc.
3447 West 130th
Cleveland, OH   44111

OREGON

Black Sheep Weaving & Craft
   Supplies
315 S.W. Third Street
Corvallis, OR   97330

Wildflower Fibres
211 N.W. Davis Street
Portland, OR   97209

TENNESSEE

The Tennessee Craftsmen
5014 North Broadway
Knoxville, TN   37917

UTAH

Intertwine
101 Trolley Square
Salt Lake City, UT   84102

Zim's
P.O. Box 7620
Salt Lake City, UT   84107

VERMONT

Weaver's Web
39 Barre Street
Montpelier, VT   05602

WASHINGTON

Northwest Cane Supply
8010 15th N.W.
Seattle, WA   98117

Northwest Looms
Box 10369
Brainbridge Island, WA   98110

WISCONSIN

Nasco Handcrafters
901 Janesville Avenue
Fort Atkinson, WI   53538

Sax Arts & Crafts
316 North Milwaukee Street
P.O. Box 2002
Milwaukee, WI   53202

INDEX

Page numbers in italics refer to material in captions or illustrations.